Gill Books
Hume Avenue, Park West, Dublin 12

www.gillbooks.ie

Gill Books is an imprint of M.H. Gill & Co.

Copyright © Teapot Press Ltd 2017

ISBN: 978-0-7171-7291-7

This book was created and produced by Teapot Press Ltd

Speeches abridged and edited by Fiona Biggs
Designed by Tony Potter & Alyssa Peacock

Printed in EU

This book is typeset in Dax and Garamond

A CIP catalogue record for this book is available
from the British Library.

5 4 3 2 1

THE POCKET
BOOK OF GREAT
IRISH
SPEECHES

INSPIRING AND PROVOCATIVE
SPEECHES FROM 1782 TO TODAY

Gill Books

Contents

Henry Grattan
(1746–1820)

Henry Grattan
1746-1820,
by Thomas
Alfred Jones,
1823-1893, after
James Ramsay,
1786-1854

Born in Dublin and educated at Trinity College, Grattan was elected as a 'Patriot' MP to the Dublin Parliament in 1775. The 1798 rebellion led to the abolition of the Dublin (known as 'Grattan's') Parliament in 1800, and in 1801 the Act of Union, creating a United Kingdom of Great Britain and Ireland, was passed. In 1805 Grattan was elected to the Parliament at Westminster, where he was a staunch advocate for Catholic emancipation. He died before it was achieved and was buried in Westminster Abbey.

'Ireland is now a nation.'

From his speech to the Irish House of Commons, Dublin, 16 April 1782

I am now to address a free people: ages have passed away, and this is the first moment in which you could be distinguished by that appellation.

I have spoken on the subject of your liberty so often, that I have nothing to add, and have only to admire by what heaven-directed steps you have proceeded until the whole faculty of the nation is braced up to the act of her own deliverance.

I found Ireland on her knees, I watched over her with a paternal solicitude; I have traced her progress from injuries to arms, and from arms to liberty. Spirit of Swift! Spirit of Molyneux! Your genius has prevailed. Ireland is now a nation. In that new character I hail her, and bowing to her august presence, I say, Esto perpetua!

She is no longer a wretched colony, returning thanks to her governor for his rapine, and to her king for his oppression; nor is she now a squabbling, fretful sectary, perplexing her little wits, and firing her furious statutes with bigotry, sophistry, disabilities and death, to transmit to posterity insignificance and war.

You, with difficulties innumerable, with dangers not a few, have done what your ancestors wished, but could not accomplish; and what your posterity may preserve, but will never equal: you have moulded the jarring elements of our country into a nation. You had not the advantages that were common to other great countries; no monuments, no trophies, none of those outward and visible signs of greatness, such as inspire mankind and connect the ambition of the age which is coming on with the example of that going off, and from the descent and the concatenation of glory: no; you have not had any great act recorded among all your misfortunes, nor have you one public tomb to assemble the crowd, and spread to the living the language of integrity and freedom.

Your historians did not supply the want of monuments; on the contrary, these narrators of your misfortunes, who should have felt for your wrongs, and have punished your oppressors with oppressions, natural scourges, the moral indignation of history, compromised with public villainy and trembled; they excited your violence, they suppressed your provocation and wrote in the chain which entrammelled their country. I am come to break that chain, and I congratulate my country, who, without any of the advantages I speak of, going forth, as it were, with nothing but a stone and a sling, and what oppression could not take away, the favour of heaven, accomplished her own redemption, and left you nothing to add and everything to admire.

The Irish House of Commons, 1780 (oil on canvas), Wheatley, Francis (1747-1801)

Theobald Wolfe Tone
(1763–1798)

Theobald Wolfe Tone was born in Dublin and studied at Trinity College. One of the co-founders of the United Irishmen in 1791, he organised a French invasion force to support a rising in Ireland in 1798, but it didn't land until after the rebellion had been quashed. Tone was tried and sentenced to death. He cut his throat on the morning scheduled for his execution and died a week later.

'It is no great effort at this day,
to add the sacrifice of my life.'

From his speech from the dock at his court martial, 10 November 1798

I mean not to give you the trouble of bringing judicial proof to convict me legally of having acted in hostility to the government of his Britannic Majesty in Ireland. I admit the fact. From my earliest youth I have regarded the connection between Great Britain and Ireland as the curse of the Irish nation, and felt convinced that, whilst it lasted, this country could never be free nor happy. My mind has been confirmed in this opinion by the experience of every succeeding year, and the conclusions which I have drawn from every fact before my eyes. In consequence, I was determined to employ all the powers which my individual efforts could move, in order to separate the two countries. That Ireland was not able of herself to throw off the yoke, I knew; I therefore sought for aid wherever it was to be found. In honourable poverty I rejected offers which, to a man in my circumstances, might be considered highly advantageous. I sought in the French Republic an ally to rescue three millions of my countrymen.

Attached to no party in the French Republic – without interest, without money, without intrigue – the openness and integrity of my views raised me to a high and confidential rank in its armies. I obtained the confidence of the Executive Directory, the approbation of my generals, and, I will venture to add, the esteem and affection of my brave comrades. When I review these circumstances, I feel a secret and internal consolation which no reverse of fortune, no sentence in the power of this court to inflict, can deprive me of, or weaken in any degree. Under the flag of the French Republic I originally engaged with a view to save and liberate my own country. For that purpose I have encountered the chances of war amongst strangers; for that purpose I repeatedly braved the terrors of the ocean, covered, as I knew it to be, with the triumphant fleets of that power which it was my glory and my duty to oppose.

I have sacrificed all my views in life; I have courted poverty; I have left a beloved wife unprotected, and children whom I adored, fatherless. After such a sacrifice in a cause which I have always considered – conscientiously considered – as the cause of justice and freedom, it is no great effort, at this day, to add the sacrifice of my life. But I hear it said that this unfortunate country has been a prey to all sorts of horrors. I sincerely lament it. I beg, however, it may be remembered that I have been absent four years from Ireland. To me these sufferings can never be attributed. I designed, by fair and open war, to procure the separation of the two countries. For open war I was prepared, but, instead of that, a system of private assassination has taken place. I repeat, whilst I deplore it, that it is not chargeable on me. Atrocities, it seems, have been committed on both sides. I do not less deplore them. I detest them from my heart; and to those who know my character and sentiments, I may safely appeal for the truth of this assertion: with them I need no justification. In a case like this, success is everything. Success, in the eyes of the vulgar, fixes its merits. Washington succeeded, and Kosciusko failed. After a combat nobly sustained – a combat which would have excited the respect and sympathy of a generous enemy – my fate has been to become a prisoner, to the eternal disgrace of those who gave the orders. I was brought here in irons like a felon. I mention this for the sake of others; for me, I am indifferent to it. I am aware of the fate which awaits me, and scorn equally the tone of complaint and that of supplication. As to the connection between this country and Great Britain, I repeat it – all that has been imputed to me (words, writings, and actions), I here deliberately avow. I have spoken and acted with reflection and on principle, and am ready to meet the consequences. Whatever be the sentence of the court, I am prepared for it. Its members will surely discharge their duty – I shall take care not to be wanting in mine.

I wish to offer a few words relative to one single point – the mode of punishment. In France our emigrés, who stand nearly in the same situation in which I now stand before you, are condemned to be shot. I ask that the court shall adjudge me the death of a soldier, and let me be shot by a platoon of grenadiers. I request this indulgence, rather in consideration of the uniform I wear, the uniform of a Chef de Brigade in the French army, than from any personal regard to myself. In order to evince my claim to this favour, I beg that the court may take the trouble to peruse my commission and letters of service in the French army. It will appear from these papers that I have not received them as a mask to cover me, but that I have been long and bona fide an officer in the French service.

John FitzGibbon, Earl of Clare
(1748–1802)

A successful barrister, John FitzGibbon was elected to the Irish House of Commons in 1778 and served as Lord Chancellor for Ireland from 1789 until his death in 1802. He was created First Earl of Clare in 1795. Firmly entrenched as a Protestant unionist, he had little regard for the Catholic population of Ireland. In 1800 he introduced the second bill to abolish the Irish Parliament, hoping to bring all power back to Westminster with the enactment of legislation creating a union between Great Britain and Ireland.

'Unless you will civilise your people,
it is vain to look for national
tranquillity or contentment.'

From his speech to the House of Lords, Dublin, 10 February 1800

We are told that by giving up a separate government, and separate Parliament, we sacrifice national dignity and independence. If gentlemen who enlarge on this theme will talk of their personal dignity and aggrandisement, I can understand them; but when I look at the squalid misery, and profound ignorance, and barbarous manners, and brutal ferocity of the mass of the Irish people, I am sickened with this rant of Irish dignity and independence. Is the dignity and independence of Ireland to consist in the continued depression and unredeemed barbarism of the great majority of the people, and the factious contentions of a puny and rapacious oligarchy, who consider the Irish nation as their political inheritance, and are ready to sacrifice the public peace and happiness to their insatiate love of patronage and power?

I hope I feel as becomes a true Irishman, for the dignity and independence of my country, and therefore I would elevate her to her proper station, in the rank of civilised nations. I wish to advance her from the degraded post of a mercenary province, to the proud station of an integral and governing member of the greatest empire in the world. I wish to withdraw the higher orders of my countrymen from the narrow and corrupted sphere of Irish politics, and to direct their attention to objects of national importance, to teach them to improve the natural energies, and extend the resources of their country, to encourage manufacturing, skill and ingenuity, and open useful channels for commercial enterprise; and above all, seriously to exert their best endeavours to tame and civilise the lower orders of the people, to inculcate in them habits of religion and morality, and industry, and due subordination, to relieve their wants, and correct their excesses; unless you will civilise your people, it is vain to look for national tranquillity or contentment.

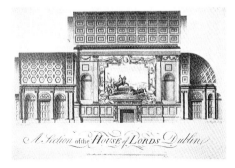

Sectional engraving of the Irish House of Lords by Peter Mazell based on the drawing by Rowland Omer, 1767.

A Section of the HOUSE of LORDS Dublin

Robert Emmet
(1778–1803)

Robert Emmet was born in Dublin and educated at Trinity College until he was excluded for expressing radical political opinions. In 1803 he organised an uprising against British rule in Ireland. It turned into a riot on the streets of Dublin and Emmet was captured, tried and sentenced to death. His oration at his trial became the stuff of legend. He was hanged in Dublin on 20 September 1803. The abysmal failure of his rebellion did not deny him a place in the pantheon of Ireland's patriot martyrs.

'Let no man write my epitaph.'

Engraving of Robert Emmet.

From his speech from the dock at Green Street, Dublin, 19 September 1803

I am asked what have I to say why sentence of death should not be pronounced upon me, according to the law. I have nothing to say that can alter your predetermination, nor that it will become me to say, with any view to the mitigation of that sentence which you are to pronounce, and I must abide by. I have much to say why my reputation should be rescued from the load of false accusation and calumny which has been cast upon it. Was I only to suffer death, after being judged guilty by your tribunal, I should bow in silence and meet the fate that awaits me without a murmur; but the sentence of the law which delivers my body to the executioner will, through the ministry of the law, labour in its own vindication, to consign my character to obloquy; for there must be guilt somewhere, whether in the sentence of the court, or in the catastrophe, time must determine.

The man dies, but his memory lives. I wish that my memory and name may animate those who survive me, while I look down with complacency on the destruction of that perfidious government which displays its power over man, as over the beasts of the forest – which sets man upon his brother, and lifts his hand, in the name of God, against the throat of his fellow who believes or doubts a little more or a little less than the government standard – a government which is steeled to barbarity by the cries of the orphans, and the tears of the widows it has made.

What, my lord, shall you tell me on the passage to the scaffold, which that tyranny has erected for my murder, that I am accountable for all the blood that has been and will be shed in this struggle of the oppressed against the oppressor – shall you tell me this, and must I be so very a slave as not to repel it? I do not fear to approach the Omnipotent Judge to answer for the conduct of my whole life; and am I to be appalled and falsified by a mere remnant of mortality here? By you, too, although, if it were possible to collect all the innocent blood that you have shed in your unhallowed ministry in one great reservoir, your lordship might swim in it.

Let no man dare, when I am dead, to charge me with dishonour; let no man attaint my memory, by believing that I could have engaged in any cause but that of my country's liberty and independence; or that I could have become the pliant minion of power, in the oppression and misery of my country. The proclamation of the provisional government speaks for our views; no inference can be tortured from it to countenance barbarity or debasement at home, or subjection, humiliation, or treachery from abroad. I would not have submitted to a foreign oppressor, for the same reason that I would resist the foreign and domestic oppressor. In the dignity of my freedom, I would have fought upon the threshold of my country, and its enemy should enter only by passing over my lifeless corpse. And am I, who lived but for my country, and who have subjected myself to the dangers of the jealous and watchful oppressor, and the bondage of the grave, only to give my countrymen their rights, and my country her independence – am I to be loaded with calumny, and not suffered to resent it? No, God forbid!

My lords, you are impatient for the sacrifice. The blood which you seek is not congealed by the artificial terrors which surround your victim; it circulates warmly and unruffled, through the channels which God created for noble purposes, but which you are bent to destroy, for purposes so grievous, that they cry to heaven. Be yet patient! I have but a few words more to say. I am going to my cold and silent grave – my lamp of life is nearly extinguished – my race is run – the grave opens to receive me, and I sink into its bosom! I have but one request to ask at my departure from this world – it is the charity of its silence! Let no man write my epitaph: for as no man who knows my motives dare now vindicate them, let not prejudice or ignorance asperse them. Let them and me repose in obscurity and peace, and my tomb remain

Execution of Robert Emmet, in Thomas Street, 20 September 1803.
Most Irishmen look idly on, while England assassinates at will! Print by J. Kirwan.

uninscribed, until other times, and other men, can do justice to my character; when my country takes her place among the nations of the earth, then, and not till then, let my epitaph be written. I have done.

Thomas Davis
(1814–1845)

Thomas Davis was a barrister by profession. He joined the Repeal Association but was frustrated by the fact that its sole platform was separatism, and by its espousal of denominational education, which mirrored that of the establishment. He was one of the first of Ireland's 'cultural' nationalists, and he was co-founder, with Charles Gavan Duffy and John Dillon, of *The Nation* newspaper in 1842. The trio were known as the Young Irelanders. Davis was just 31 when he caught scarlet fever and died.

'Seek to take your country forward.'

From his speech to the 'Hist', Trinity College Dublin, 17 June 1839

Gentlemen, the Dublin University is the laughing stock of the literary world, and an obstacle to the nation's march; its inaccessible library and effete system of instruction render it ridiculous abroad; add its unaccounted funds, and its bigot laws, and know why it is hated.

But, gentlemen, you have a country! The people among whom we were born, with whom we live, for whom, if our minds are in health, we have most sympathy, or those over whom we have power – power to make them wise, great, good. Reason points out our native land as the field for our exertions, and tells us that without patriotism a profession of benevolence is the cloak of the selfish man; and does not sentiment confirm the decree of reason? The country of our birth, our education, of our recollections, ancestral, personal, national; the country of our loves, our friendships, our hopes; our country: the cosmopolite is unnatural, base – I would fain say, impossible. To act on a world is for those above it, not of it. Patriotism is human philanthropy.

Gentlemen, many of you possess, more of you are growing into possession of, great powers – powers which were given you for good, which you may use for evil. I trust that not as adventurers, or rash meddlers, will you enter on public life. But to enter on it in some way or other the state of mind in Ireland will compel you. You must act as citizens, and it is well, 'non nobis solum nati sumus, ortusque nostri partem patria vindicat' [*We are not born for ourselves alone but our country claims a share of our being – Plato*]. Patriotism once felt to be a duty becomes so. To act in politics is a matter of duty everywhere; here, of necessity. To make that action honourable to yourselves, and serviceable to your country, is a matter of choice. In your public career you will be solicited by a thousand temptations to sully your souls with the gold and place of a foreign court, or the transient breath of a dishonest popularity; dishonest, when adverse to the good, though flattering to the prejudices of the people.

But if neither the present nor the past can rouse you, let the sun of hope, the beams of the future, awake you to exertion in the cause of patriotism. Seek, oh seek to make your country not behind at least in the progress of the nations. Education, the apostle of progress, hath gone forth. Knowledge is not virtue, but may be rendered its precursor. Virtue is not alone enjoyment, is not all happiness; but be sure, when the annunciation of virtue comes, the advent of happiness is at hand. Seek to take your country forward in her progress to that goal, where she, in common with the other nations, may hear the annunciation of virtue, and share that advent of happiness, holiness and peace.

Trinity College, Dublin, Ireland. Line engraving after J. Ja Wellcome

Daniel O'Connell
(1775–1847)

Daniel O'Connell, 'the Liberator', was born in Kerry. The driving force behind the movement for Catholic emancipation (he was elected MP for Clare in 1828 but was precluded from taking his seat because he was a Catholic), he was famous for his spectacular 'monster meetings' at which he addressed huge crowds. Catholic emancipation was granted in 1829 and O'Connell became involved in the unsuccessful campaign to repeal the Union. A devout Catholic, he died in 1847 in Genoa, Italy, while on pilgrimage to Rome, and was buried in Glasnevin Cemetery. His heart was buried in Rome.

'O my friends, it is a country
worth fighting for.'

From his speech at a 'monster meeting', Mullaghmast, County Kildare, 1 October 1843

A t Tara I protested against the Union – I repeat the protest at Mullaghmast. I declare solemnly my thorough conviction as a constitutional lawyer, that the Union is totally void in point of principle and of constitutional force. I tell you that no portion of the empire had the power to traffic on the rights and liberties of the Irish people. The Irish people nominated them to make laws, and not legislatures. They were appointed to act under the Constitution, and not annihilate it. Their delegation from the people was confined within the limits of the Constitution, and the moment the Irish Parliament went beyond those limits and destroyed the Constitution, that moment it annihilated its own power, but could not annihilate the immortal spirit of liberty which belongs, as a rightful inheritance, to the people of Ireland. Take it, then, from me that the Union is void.

I admit there is the force of a law, because it has been supported by the policeman's truncheon, by the soldier's bayonet, and by the horseman's sword; because it is supported by the courts of law and those who have power to adjudicate in them; but I say solemnly, it is not supported by constitutional right. The Union, therefore, in my thorough conviction, is totally void, and I avail myself of this opportunity to announce to several hundreds of thousands of my fellow subjects that the Union is an unconstitutional law and that it is not fated to last long – its hour is approaching.

O my friends, I will keep you clear of all treachery – there shall be no bargain, no compromise with England – we shall take nothing but repeal, and a Parliament in College Green. You will never, by my advice, confide in any false hopes they hold out to you; never confide in anything coming from them, or cease from your struggle, no matter what promise may be held to you, until you hear me say I am satisfied; and I will tell you where I will say that – near the statue of King William, in College Green. No; we came here to express our determination to die to a man, if necessary, in the cause of old Ireland. We came to take advice of each other, and, above all, I believe you came here to take my advice. I can tell you, I have the game in my hand – I have the triumph secure – I have the repeal certain, if you but obey my advice.

I will go slow – you must allow me to do so – but you will go sure. No man shall find himself imprisoned or persecuted who follows my advice. I have led you thus far in safety; I have swelled the multitude of repealers until they are identified with the entire population, or nearly the entire population, of the land, for seven-eighths of the Irish people are now enrolling themselves repealers. I do not want more power; I have power enough; and all I ask of you is to allow me to use it. I will go on quietly and slowly, but I will go on firmly, and with a certainty of success.

Yes, you have those high qualities – religious fidelity, continuous love of country. Even your enemies admit that the world has never produced any people that exceeded the Irish in activity and strength. The Scottish philosopher has declared, and the French philosopher has confirmed it, that number one in the human race is, blessed be Heaven, the Irishman. In moral virtue, in religion, in perseverance, and in glorious temperance, you excel. Have I any teetotallers here? Yes, it is teetotalism that is repealing the Union. I could not afford to bring you together, I would not dare to bring you together, but that I had the teetotallers for my police.

Yes, among the nations of the earth, Ireland stands number one in the physical strength of her sons and in the beauty and purity of her daughters. Ireland, land of my forefathers, how my mind expands, and my spirit walks abroad in something of majesty, when I contemplate the high qualities, inestimable virtues, and true purity and piety and religious fidelity of the inhabitants of your green fields and productive mountains. Oh, what a scene surrounds us! It is not only the countless thousands of brave and active and peaceable and religious men that are here assembled, but Nature herself has written her character with the finest beauty in the verdant plains that surround us.

Let any man run around the horizon with his eye, and tell me if created nature ever produced anything so green and so lovely, so undulating, so teeming with production. The richest harvests that any land can produce are those reaped in Ireland; and then here are the sweetest meadows, the greenest fields, the loftiest mountains, the purest streams, the noblest rivers, the most capacious harbours – and her water power is equal to turn the machinery of the whole world. O my friends, it is a country worth fighting for – it is a country worth dying for; but, above all, it is a country worth being tranquil, determined, submissive and docile for; disciplined as you are in obedience to those who are breaking the way, and trampling down the barriers between you and your constitutional liberty, I will see every man of you having a vote, and every man protected by the ballot from the agent or landlord. I will see labour protected, and every title to possession recognised, when you are industrious and honest. I will see prosperity again throughout your land – the busy hum of the shuttle and the tinkling of the smithy shall be heard again. We shall see the nailer employed even until the middle of the night, and the carpenter covering himself with his chips. I will see prosperity in all its gradations spreading through a happy, contented, religious land. I will hear the hymn of a happy people go forth at sunrise to God in praise of His mercies – and I will see the evening sun set down among the uplifted hands of a religious and free population. Every blessing that man can bestow and religion can confer upon the faithful heart shall spread throughout the land. Stand by me – join with me – I will say be obedient to me, and Ireland shall be free.

Daniel O'Connell proposing
the formation of the
Catholic Association, 1825.

Charles Stewart Parnell
(1846–1891)

Born into a wealthy Anglo-Irish family in County Wicklow, Charles Stewart Parnell is best remembered for his tireless campaigning for Home Rule for Ireland. In 1885, when the Liberal Party's Joseph Chamberlain proposed a compromise deal of greater autonomy that didn't go as far as granting Home Rule, Parnell addressed a Home Rule rally in Cork. As a result of his efforts, Prime Minister William Gladstone introduced the first Home Rule Bill later that year. A personal scandal destroyed Parnell's career and health and he died at the age of 45.

'No man has a right to say to his country,
"Thus far shalt thou go and no further".'

From a speech in Cork, 21 January 1885

At the election in 1880 I laid certain principles before you and you accepted them. I said and I pledged myself, that I should form one of an independent Irish party to act in opposition to every English government which refused to concede the just rights of Ireland. And the longer time which is gone by since then, the more I am convinced that that is the true policy to pursue so far as parliamentary policy is concerned, and that it will be impossible for either or both of the English parties to contend for any long time against a determined band of Irishmen acting honestly upon these principles, and backed by the Irish people.

But we have not alone had that object view – we have always been very careful not to fetter or control the people at home in any way, not to prevent them from doing anything by their own strength which it is possible for them to do. Sometimes, perhaps, in our anxiety in this direction we have asked them to do what is beyond their strength, but I hold that it is better even to encourage you to do what is beyond your strength even should you fail sometimes in the attempt than to teach you to be subservient and unreliant. You have been encouraged to organise yourselves, to depend upon the rectitude of your cause for your justification, and to depend upon the determination which has helped Irishmen through many centuries to retain the name of Ireland and to retain her nationhood.

Nobody could point to any single action of ours in the House of Commons or out of it which was not based upon the knowledge that behind us existed a strong and brave people, that without the help of the people our exertions would be as nothing, and that with their help and with their confidence we should be, as I believe we shall prove to be in the near future, invincible and unconquerable.

I come back – and every Irish politician must be forcibly driven back – to the consideration of the great question of national self-government for Ireland. I do not know how this great question will be eventually settled. I do not know whether England will be wise in time and concede to constitutional arguments and methods the restitution of that which was stolen from us towards the close of the last century. It is given to none of us to forecast the future, and just as it is impossible for us to say in what way or by what means the national question may be settled, in what way full justice may be done to Ireland, so it is impossible for us to say to what extent that justice should be done. We cannot ask for less than restitution of Grattan's Parliament. No man has a right to say to his country, 'Thus far shalt thou go and no further'; and we have never attempted to fix the ne plus ultra to the progress of Ireland's nationhood, and we never shall.

But gentlemen, while we leave those things to time, circumstances and the future, we must each one of us resolve in our own hearts that we shall at all times do everything which within us lies to obtain for Ireland the fullest measure of her rights. In this way we shall avoid difficulties and contentions amongst each other. In this way we shall not give up anything which the future may put in favour of our country, and while we struggle today for that which may seem possible for us with our combination, we must struggle for it with the proud consciousness, and that we shall not do anything to hinder or prevent better men who may come after us from gaining better things than those for which we now contend.

Michael Davitt

(1846–1906)

Michael Davitt was born to a poor Catholic family in County Mayo. When his family was evicted his parents decided to move to England where the nine-year-old Davitt was maimed in a factory accident. In 1865 he joined the Fenians and was imprisoned for treason-felony in 1870. In 1877 he founded the Land League in his home county and brought Parnell and the Fenians together. He was accused of having been responsible for a campaign that led to the notorious Phoenix Park murders in 1882. In 1887 he gave an eloquent address to a special commission of enquiry set up to consider the allegations. It was both an eloquent defence of the Land League and an attack on landlordism.

*'All distrust and opposition will
die out of the Irish heart.'*

Unflattering depiction of Michael Davitt by John D.
Reigh in *United Ireland*, a pro-Parnell newspaper, 1892

"I WILL BE FAITHFUL
TO HER MAJESTY,
HER HEIRS & SUCCESSORS,
ACCORDING TO LAW,
SO HELP ME, GOD."

From his speech to the Special Irish Commission investigating the Phoenix Park murders, 29 October 1889

I can only say that I represent the working classes of my country here as I did in the Land League movement, and I know how they feel, as I do, that, no matter how bitter past memories have rankled in our hearts, no matter how much we have suffered in the past in person or in our country's cause, no matter how fiercely some of us have fought against and denounced the injustice of alien misgovernment: I know that, before a feeling of kindness and of good will on the part of the people of England, Scotland and Wales, and in a belief in their awakening sense of justice towards our country, all distrust and opposition and bitter recollections will die out of the Irish heart, and the Anglo-Irish strife will terminate forever when landlordism and Castle rule are dethroned by Great Britain's verdict for reason and for right.

Whatever legal points are to occupy your lordships' study and care in this long and arduous investigation, it will appear to the public that two institutions stood indicted before it.

One has had a life of centuries, the other an existence of but a few brief years. They are charged, respectively, by the accused and the accusers, with the responsibility for the agrarian crimes of the period covered by this inquiry.

One is Irish landlordism, the other is the Irish Land League. *The Times* alleges that the young institution is the culprit. The Land League, through me, its founder, repels the accusation, and counter-charges landlordism with being the instigation and the cause, not alone of the agrarian violence and crimes from 1879 to 1887, but of all which are on record, from the times spoken of by Spenser and Davis in the days of Elizabeth down to the date of this commission.

To prove this real and hoary-headed culprit guilty I have not employed or purchased the venal talent of a forger, or offered the tempting price of liberty for incriminatory evidence to unhappy convicts in penal cells. Neither have I brought convicted assassins or professional perjurers before your lordships. Nor have I had to scour the purlieus of American cities for men who would sell evidence that might repair the case which Richard Pigott's confession destroyed, and which his self-inflicted death has sealed with tragic emphasis.

But there is another and a higher interest involved in the drama of this commission now rapidly drawing to a close; an interest far surpassing in importance, and the possible consequences of your lordships' judgment, anything else comprised in this investigation. It stands between *The Times* and landlordism on the one hand; the persons here charged and the Land League on the other. In bygone ages historians, with some prophetic instinct, called it 'The Isle of Destiny'.

And Destiny seems to have reserved it for a career of trial, of suffering, and of sorrow. That same Destiny has linked this country close to England. Politically it has remained there for 700 years or more. During that period few people ever placed upon this earth have experienced more injustice or more criminal neglect at the hands of their rulers than we have.

This even English history will not and dare not deny. This land so tried and treated has nevertheless struggled, generation after generation, now with one means, now with another, to widen the sphere of its contracted religious, social and political liberties – liberties so contracted by the deliberate policy of its English governing power; and ever and always were these struggles made against the prejudice and might, and often the cruelties of this same power, backed by the support of the indifference of the British nation.

But despite all this, the cause so fought and upheld has ever and always succeeded sooner or later, in vindicating its underlying principles of truth and justice, and in winning from the power which failed to crush them an after-justification of their righteous demands.

A people so persevering in its fight for the most priceless and most cherished of human and civil rights, so opposed, but so invariably vindicated, might surely in these days of progress and of enlightenment excite in the breasts of Englishmen other feelings than those of jealousy, hate, revenge and fear. To many, thank God, it has appealed successfully at last to what is good and what is best in English nature. It has spoken to the spirit of Liberty, and has turned the love of justice in the popular mind towards Ireland, and has asked the British people, in the interests of peace, to put force and mistrust away with every other abandoned weapon of Ireland's past misrule, and to place in their stead the soothing and healing remedies of confidence and friendship, based upon reason and equality.

John Dillon
(1851–1927)

John Dillon was born in Dublin, a son of Young Irelander John Blake Dillon. He was a Home Rule MP, but when public opinion turned against Parnell he led the movement instigated against him at Westminster. Dillon was a staunch supporter of Gladstone, who introduced several Home Rule Bills. Dillon's tribute to him on his death reflected the high esteem in which the 'grand old man' of British politics was held in Ireland. Dillon led the Irish Party for a few months in 1918 after John Redmond's death, but retired from political life when he lost his seat to the Sinn Féin candidate.

'Mr Gladstone was the greatest
Englishman of his time.'

From his speech to the House of Commons, Westminster, 20 May 1898

As an Irishman I feel that I have a special right to join in paying a tribute to the great Englishman who died yesterday, because the last and, as all men will agree, the most glorious years of his strenuous and splendid life were dominated by the love which he bore to our nation, and by the eager and even passionate desire to serve Ireland and give her liberty and peace.

By virtue of the splendid quality of his nature, which seemed to give him perpetual youth, Mr Gladstone's faith in a cause to which he had once devoted himself never wavered, nor did his enthusiasm grow cold. Difficulties and the weight of advancing years were alike ineffectual to blunt the edge of his purpose or to daunt his splendid courage, and even when racked with pain, and when the shadow of death was darkening over him, his heart still yearned towards the people of Ireland, and his last public utterance was a message of sympathy for Ireland and of hope for her future.

His was a great and deep nature. He loved the people with a wise and persevering love. His love of the people and his abiding faith in the efficacy of liberty and of government based on the consent of the people, as an instrument of human progress, was not the outcome of youthful enthusiasm, but the deep-rooted growth of long years, and drew its vigour from an almost unparalleled experience of men and of affairs. Above all men I have ever known or read of, in his case the lapse of years seemed to have no influence to narrow his sympathies or to contract his heart. Young men felt old beside him. And to the last no generous cause, no suffering people appealed to him in vain, and that glorious voice which had so often inspired the friends of freedom and guided them to victory was the last at the service of the weak and the oppressed of whatever race or nation. Mr Gladstone was the greatest Englishman of his time.

He loved his own people as much as any Englishman that ever lived. But through communion with the hearts of his own people he acquired that wider and greater gift – the power of understanding and sympathising with other peoples. He entered into their sorrows and felt for their oppressions. And with splendid courage he did not hesitate, even in the case of his much-loved England, to condemn her when he thought she was wronging others, and in so doing he fearlessly faced odium and unpopularity among his own people, which must have been bitter for him to bear; and so he became something far greater than a British statesman, and took a place amid the greatest leaders of the human race. Amid the obstructions and the cynicism of a materialistic age he never lost his hold on the 'ideal'. And so it came to pass that wherever throughout the civilised world a race or nation of men were suffering from oppression, their thoughts turned towards Gladstone, and when that mighty voice was raised in their behalf Europe and the civilised world listened, and the breathing of new hopes entered into the hearts of men made desperate by long despair.

In the years that have gone by England has lost many men who served their country splendidly and round whose graves the British people deeply mourned; but round the deathbed of Gladstone the people of this island are joined in their sorrow by many peoples, and today throughout the Christian world – in many lands and in many tongues – prayers will be offered to that God on whom in his last supreme hour of trial Mr Gladstone humbly placed his firm reliance, begging that He will remember to His great servant how ardently he loved his fellow men, without distinction of race, while he lived among them, and how mightily he laboured for their good.

Constance Markievicz
(1868–1927)

Constance Gore-Booth was born in London into the Ango-Irish Protestant ascendancy. She studied art in London and married a Polish count, Casimir Dunin Markievicz. She developed an interest in women's suffrage and active Irish nationalism, joining Sinn Féin and the Daughters of Ireland. During the Lockout in 1913 she provided aid to striking Dublin workers and their families, and in 1916 she participated in the rising, fighting in St Stephen's Green. She was sentenced to death but reprieved. She became the first female MP elected to the House of Commons, but she took her seat instead in the First Dáil in 1919, serving as minister for labour.

'Now, here is a chance for our women.'

From her speech to the Students' National Literacy Society, Dublin, 1909

I take it as a great compliment that so many of you, the rising young women of Ireland, who are distinguishing yourselves every day and coming more and more to the front, should give me this opportunity. We older people look to you with great hope and a great confidence that in your gradual emancipation you are bringing fresh ideas, fresh energies and above all a great genius for sacrifice into the life of the nation.

Lately things seem to be changing … a strong tide of liberty seems to be coming towards us, swelling and growing and carrying before it all the outposts that hold women enslaved and bearing them triumphantly into the life of the nation to which they belong.

Women, from having till very recently stood so far removed from all politics, should be able to formulate a much clearer and more incisive view of the political situation than men. For a man from the time he is a mere lad is more or less in touch with politics, and has usually the label of some party attached to him, long before he properly understands what it really means.

Now, here is a chance for our women. Fix your mind on the ideal of Ireland free, with her women enjoying the full rights of citizenship in their own nation, and no one will be able to sidetrack you, and so make use of you to use up the energies of the nation in obtaining all sorts of concessions – concessions too, that for the most part were coming in the natural course of evolution, and were perhaps just hastened a few years by the fierce agitations to obtain them.

You will go out into the world and get elected onto as many public bodies as possible, and by degree through your exertions no public institution – whether hospital, workhouse, asylum or any other, and no private house – but will be supporting the industries of your country.

Tommy Moore, the popular poet of his day and also many days later, has set Ireland a very low ideal of woman to worship. To him, woman is merely sex and an excuse for a drink. Not a companion or a friend, but a beautiful houri holding dominion by her careful manipulation of her sex and her good looks.

The better ideal for women who, whether they like it or not, are living in a work-a-day world, would be – If you want to walk around Ireland, or any other country, dress suitably in short skirts and strong boots, leave your jewels and gold wands in the bank, and buy a revolver. Don't trust to your 'feminine charm' and your capacity for getting on the soft side of men, but take up your responsibilities and be prepared to go your own way, depending for safety on your own courage, your own truth and your own common sense, and not on the problematic chivalry of the men you may meet on the way.

A consciousness of their own dignity and worth should be encouraged in women. They should be urged to get away from wrong ideals and false standards of womanhood, to escape from their domestic ruts, their feminine pens. We have got to get rid of the last vestige of the Harem before woman is free as our dream of the future would have her.

Countess Markievicz posing with her pistol.

James Larkin
(1874–1947)

James Larkin was born in Liverpool to Irish parents and was raised by his grandparents in Newry. He returned to Liverpool aged 12 and worked as a docks labourer. He joined the dockers' union and went to Belfast and Dublin to organise for the union, then formed the Irish Transport and General Workers' Union. In 1912 he co-founded the Irish Labour Party with Connolly and the Irish Citizen Army in 1913. He encouraged Irishmen not to fight for the British in the First World War. He was in the US when the Rising took place. In 1924 he set up the Irish Workers' Union and was elected to the Dáil in 1932.

'If they want war, then war they will have.'

From his speech to the Board of Trade's tribunal of inquiry into the Dublin Lockout, 4 October 1913

The first point I want to make is that the employers in this city, and throughout Ireland generally, have put forward a claim that they have a right to deal with their own; that they have a right to use and exploit individuals as they please; that they have duties which they limit, and they have responsibilities which they also limit, in their operation. They take to themselves that they have all the rights that are given to men and to societies of men, but they deny the right of the men to claim that they also have a substantial claim on the share of the produce they produce, and they further say that they want no third party interference. They want to deal with their workingmen individually. They say that they are men of such paramount intelligence and so able in their organising ability as captains of industry, who can always carry on their business in their own way, and they deny the right of the men and women who work for them to combine and try to assist one another in trying to improve their conditions of life.

Let people who desire to know the truth go to the factories and see the maimed girls, the weak and sickly, whose eyes are being put out and their bodies scarred and their souls seared and when they were no longer able to be useful enough to gain their £1 a week, or whatever wage they earned, were thrown into the human scrap heap. These things were to be found in their midst, and yet the people who caused these conditions of wretchedness described workingmen as loafers.

I am concerned in something greater, something better, and something holier – a mutual relation between those carrying on industry in Ireland. These men (the employers) with their limited intelligence cannot see that. I cannot help that. I cannot compel them to look at the thing from my point of view. It is not to our interest to have men locked out or on strike. We don't get double wages. They say 'Larkin is making £18 a week', and has made more than £18 a week, but he never got it unfortunately. I have lived among the working classes all my life. I have starved because men denied me food. I worked very hard at a very early age. I had no opportunities like the men opposite, but whatever opportunities I got I have availed of them. I am called anti-Christ and an atheist. If I were an atheist I would not deny it. I am a socialist and have always claimed to be a socialist.

I believe in a co-operative commonwealth. That is a long way ahead in Ireland. Why cannot I help as you can help in working the present system in a proper, reasonable way, conducive to both sides, and I have suggested the machinery that may be put into operation.

Can anyone say one word against me as a man? Can they make any disparagement of my character? Have I lessened the standard of life? Have I demoralised anyone? Is there something in my private life or my public life of which I should feel ashamed? These men denounced me from the pulpit, and say I am making £18 a week and that I have a mansion in Dublin.

When the position of the workers in Dublin was taken into consideration, was it any wonder that there was a necessity for a Larkin to arise, and if there was one thing more than another in my life of which I will always be proud it was the part I have taken in rescuing the workers of Dublin from the brutalising and degrading conditions under which they laboured.

We are out to break down racial and sectarian barriers. My suggestion to the employers is that if they want peace we are prepared to meet them, but if they want war, then war they will have.

Proclamation issued by E.G. Swift, Magistrate of the Dublin Metropolitan Police District, in an attempt to stop the huge public meeting that Larkin had called for, planned to take place on Sackville Street on Sunday 31 August 1913. Larkin publicly burned the proclamation.

A PROCLAMATION

WHEREAS it has been represented to me, being a Justice of the Peace in and for the County of the City of Dublin by, an information duly sworn, that a number of persons will meet or assemble at

SACKVILLE STREET
OR ITS NEIGHBOURHOOD
in the said County of the City of Dublin, on or about

the 31st day of AUGUST, 1913

and that the object of such Meeting or Assemblage is seditious, and that the said Meeting or Assemblage would cause terror and alarm to, and dissension between, His Majesty's subjects, and would be an unlawful assembly.

NOW I do hereby prohibit such Meeting or Assemblage, and do strictly caution and forewarn all Persons whomsoever that they do abstain from taking part in or encouraging or inciting to the same.

AND I do hereby give notice that if in defiance of this Proclamation any such Meeting or Assemblage at Sackville Street or its neighbourhood shall be attempted or take place, the same will be prevented and all Persons attempting to take part in or encouraging the same, or inciting thereto, will be proceeded against according to law.

AND I do hereby enjoin all Magistrates and Officers intrusted with the preservation of the Public Peace, and all others whom it may concern, to aid and assist in the due and proper execution of the Law in preventing any such Meeting or Assemblage as aforesaid, and in the effectual dispersion and suppression of the same, and in the detection and prosecution of those who after this Notice, shall offend in the respects aforesaid.

Given under my hand this 29th day of August, 1913.

E. G. SWIFTE,
Chief Divisional Magistrate, Dublin Metropolitan Police District.

GOD SAVE THE KING.

Edward Carson
(1854–1935)

Born in Dublin into an Anglo-Irish family, Edward Carson was one of the most celebrated barristers of his day. In 1892 he was elected to the House of Commons where he was the leader of the parliamentary unionists from 1910 to 1921. He was vehemently opposed to Home Rule for Ireland and was instrumental in organising the Ulster Solemn League and Covenant in 1912. In 1914 the King's speech to the Houses of Parliament laid the ground for the enactment of the latest Home Rule Bill under Prime Minister Asquith.

'Ulster is asking to be let alone.'

From his response to the King's speech, Westminster, 11 February 1914

What is the first lesson that we deduce or learn from this grave statement in His Majesty's speech? We have been two years discussing this question, and I certainly have been two years trying to make the position of the loyalists of Ireland known, and now, after two years, the first lesson we learn is this, that the bill of the government, on their own confession, has utterly failed to find a solution of the Irish question.

They are always talking of concessions to Ulster. Ulster is not asking for concessions. Ulster is asking to be let alone. When you talk of concession, what you really mean is, 'We want to lay down what is the minimum of wrong we can do to Ulster.' Let me tell you that the results of two years' delay and the treatment we have received during these two years have made your task and made our task far more difficult. You have driven these men to enter into a covenant for their mutual protection. No doubt you have laughed at their covenant. Have a good laugh at it now. Well, so far as I am concerned, I am not the kind of man who will go over to Ulster one day and say, 'Enter into a covenant,' and go over the next day and say, 'Break it.' But there is something more. You have insulted them.

Believe me, whatever way you settle the Irish question, there are only two ways to deal with Ulster. It is for statesmen to say which is the best and right one. She is not a part of the community which can be bought. She will not allow herself to be sold. You must therefore either coerce her if you go on, or you must, in the long run, by showing that good government can come under the home rule bill, try and win her over to the case of the rest of Ireland. You probably can coerce her – although I doubt it. If you do, what will be the disastrous consequences not only to Ulster, but to this country and the Empire? Will my fellow countryman, the leader of the Nationalist Party, have gained anything? I will agree with him – I do not believe he wants to triumph any more than I do. But will he have gained anything if he takes over these people and then applies for what he used to call – at all events his party used to call – the enemies of the people to come in and coerce them into obedience? No, sir, one false step in relation to Ulster will, in my opinion, render for ever impossible a solution of the Irish question. You have never alleged, and can never allege, that this bill gives her one atom of advantage. Nay, you cannot deny that it takes away many advantages that she has as a constituent part of the

Banner probably reads: 'We will not have home rule for Ireland.'

United Kingdom. You cannot deny that in the past she had produced the most loyal and law-abiding part of the citizens of Ireland. After all that, for these two years, every time we came before you your only answer to us – the majority of you, at all events – was to insult us, and to make little of us. I say to the leader of the Nationalist Party, if you want Ulster, go and take her, or go and win her.

James Connolly
(1868–1916)

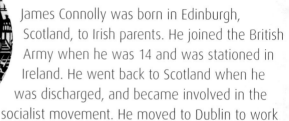

James Connolly was born in Edinburgh, Scotland, to Irish parents. He joined the British Army when he was 14 and was stationed in Ireland. He went back to Scotland when he was discharged, and became involved in the socialist movement. He moved to Dublin to work for the Dublin Socialist Club (later the Irish Socialist Republican Party) in 1896. He founded the Irish Labour Party in 1912 and set up the Irish Citizen Army in 1913 to defend the striking Dublin workers. He agreed to combine forces with the Irish Volunteers for the 1916 Rising. As one of its leaders, he was executed on 12 May 1916.

'If ever you shoulder a rifle,
let it be for Ireland.'

From his speech at a meeting in Dublin on 30 August 1914, to commemorate the deaths of three comrades killed during the Dublin Lockout

They were murdered for the sake of great principles. It had not been a mere casual murder, but a cold-blooded and premeditated one, deliberately planned with the idea in mind that as they went to their graves, so went the hopes for which they fought. When they were murdered all the hopes of the Irish workers would be slain with them; when they were foully done to death all our aspirations for a cleaner, better city and grander nation would be murdered, too.

Where do we stand today? The Irish Transport and General Workers' Union and the hopes of the Irish working class, and that class itself stands erect and resolute, fearing no man, and the British Government is down on its knees praying for the Russians to come and save them. Our fight of last year was not for added wages and reduction of hours; it was for an opportunity of building up in our midst men and women, a chance to develop nobility and grandeur of character for men and women, a time to realise the nobility of life, to study the history of Ireland, to study our rights as well as our duties; time to develop men and women for the coming crisis, so that they might take advantage of it when it came. Abject servility there is in Ireland; whatever of the spirit of a slave that in you lies, lies with those who served to cripple the grandest movement ever started. If labour controlled your destinies, conjure the picture of what might have happened when, after Gray and Asquith had plunged England into war, there arose a clamour for Redmond. And Redmond, without consulting you, the people of Ireland, pledged us to war with as kindly, gracious a nation as God ever put the breath of life into – what happened then? Redmond when they shouted for him might have sat still and let them shout, then before another sun rose got a measure greater than Grattan dreamed of. Redmond, as spokesman of the majority of the Irish people might have risen and said: 'I and my colleagues will go to Ireland and consult the Irish Nation.' Then would Ireland be a nation in reality. 'We have waited and now Germany has come, and we will start our own Parliament. Stop us if you can.' Help would have come from all sides. Why the R.I.C. would have acted as a guard of honour!

These men have sold you. Sold you? No, by God, given you away. Whether my speech is pro-German or pro-Irish, I don't know. As an Irish worker I owe a duty to our class; counting no allegiance to the Empire; I'd be glad to see it back in the bottomless pit. The Irish workers hold themselves ready to bargain with whoever can make a bargain. England has been fighting Germany. If it were not for the Russians, French and Japanese, the British would not have made a mouthful for the Germans. The Germans are in Boulogne, where Napoleon projected an invasion of Britain. To Ireland is only a twelve hours' run. If you are itching for a rifle, itching to fight, have a country of your own; better to fight for our own country than for the robber empire. If ever you shoulder a rifle, let it be for Ireland. Conscription or no conscription, they will never get me or mine. You have been told you are not strong, that you have no rifles. Revolutions do not start with rifles; start first and get your rifles after. Our curse is our belief in our weakness. We are not weak, we are strong. Make up your mind to strike before your opportunity goes.

John Redmond

(1856–1918)

John Redmond was born in County Wexford, son of the local MP. Elected as an MP in 1880, he led the anti-Parnellites after Parnell's death and when war broke out in Europe in 1914 he promised that the Volunteers would defend Britain, causing a split in the movement. The original Volunteer movement collapsed and was replaced by the Irish Volunteers, which fought in the 1916 Rising. Most Irish people were supportive of Redmond's move, but others thought he was betraying Ireland's bid for nationhood, at a time when Home Rule had been put on hold for the duration of the war.

'This war is undertaken in defence of the highest principles of religion and morality.'

John Redmond, pictured with his wife and probably his daughter, around 1914. He was leader of the Irish parliamentary party from 1908 to 1918.

From a speech to the Volunteers at Woodenbridge, County Wicklow, 20 September 1914

Fellow countrymen, it was fortunate chance that enabled me to be present here today. I was motoring past, and I did not know until I arrived here that this gathering of the Volunteers was to take place at Woodenbridge. I could not deny myself the pleasure and honour of waiting to meet you, to meet so many of those whom I have personally known for many long years, and to see them fulfilling a high duty to their country. I have no intention of making a speech. All I desire to say to you is that I congratulate you upon the favourable beginning of the work you have made.

You have only barely made a beginning. You will yet have hard work before you can call yourselves efficient soldiers, and you will have to have in your hand – every man – as efficient weapons as I am glad to see in the hands of some, at any rate, of your numbers. Looking back as I naturally do, upon the history of Wicklow, I know that you will make efficient soldiers. Efficient soldiers for what?

Wicklow Volunteers, in spite of the peaceful happiness and beauty of the scene in which we stand, remember this country at this moment is in a state of war, and your duty is a twofold duty. The duty of the manhood of Ireland is twofold. Its duty is, at all costs, to defend the shores of Ireland against foreign invasion. It is a duty more than that of taking care that Irish valour proves itself; on the field of war it has always proved itself in the past. The interests of Ireland – of the whole of Ireland – are at stake in this war. This war is undertaken in the defence of the highest principles of religion and morality and right, and it would be a disgrace for ever to our country and a reproach to her manhood and a denial of the lessons of her history if young Ireland confined their efforts to remaining at home to defend the shores of Ireland from an unlikely invasion, and to shrinking from the duty of proving on the field of battle that gallantry and courage which has distinguished our race all through history. I say to you, therefore, your duty is twofold. I am glad to see such magnificent material for soldiers around me, and I say to you: go on drilling and make yourselves efficient for the work, and then account yourselves as men, not only for Ireland itself, but wherever the fighting line extends, in defence of right, of freedom and religion in this war.

Pádraig Pearse
(1979–1916)

Pádraig Pearse was born in Dublin and was called to the Irish bar in 1901. He became a director of the Gaelic League, founded in 1893 to promote the Irish language. He became a member of the provisional committee of the Irish Volunteers on their formation in 1913. He was unenthusiastic about the limited independence promised by Home Rule. He was a talented and rousing public speaker and he put his abilities to good use at the funeral of the great Fenian, Jeremiah O'Donovan Rossa in 1915. As one of the main movers of the Easter Rising, Pearse was executed on 3 May 1916.

'From the graves of patriot men and women spring living nations.'

Patrick Pearse (litho), Irish School, (20th century)

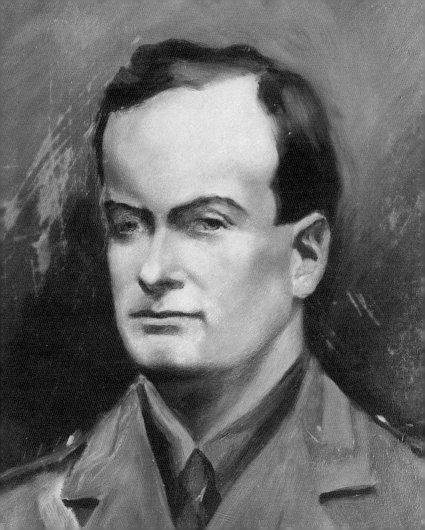

Oration at Jeremiah O'Donovan Rossa's funeral, Glasnevin Cemetery, Dublin, 1 August 1915

It has seemed right, before we turn away from this place in which we have hid the mortal remains of O'Donovan Rossa, that one among us should, in the name of all, speak the praise of that valiant man, and endeavour to formulate the thought and the hope that are in us as we stand around his grave. And if there is anything that makes it fitting that I, rather than some other, I rather than one of the grey-haired men who were young with him and shared in his labour and in his suffering, should speak here, it is perhaps that I may be taken as speaking on behalf of a new generation that has been rebaptised in the Fenian faith, and that has accepted the responsibility of carrying out the Fenian programme. I propose to you then that, here by the grave of this unrepentant Fenian, we renew our baptismal vows; that, here by the grave of this unconquered and unconquerable man, we ask of God, each one for himself, such unshakeable purpose, such high and gallant courage, such unbreakable strength of soul as belonged to O'Donovan Rossa.

Deliberately here we avow ourselves, as he avowed himself in the dock, Irishmen of one allegiance only. We of the Irish volunteers, and you others who are associated with us in today's task and duty, are bound together and must stand together henceforth in brotherly union of the achievement of the freedom of Ireland. And we know only one definition of freedom: it is Tone's definition, it is Mitchel's definition, it is Rossa's definition. Let no man blaspheme the cause that the dead generations of Ireland served by giving it any other name and definition than their name and definition.

We stand at Rossa's grave not in sadness but rather in exaltation of spirit that has been given to us to come thus into so close a communion with that brave and splendid Gael. Splendid and holy causes are served by men who are themselves splendid and holy. O'Donovan Rossa was splendid in the proud manhood of him, splendid in the heroic grace of him, splendid in the Gaelic strength and clarity and truth of him. And all that splendour and pride and strength was compatible with a humility and a simplicity of devotion to Ireland, to all that was olden and beautiful and Gaelic in Ireland, the holiness and simplicity of patriotism of a Michael O'Clery or of an Eoghan O'Growney. The clear true eyes of this man almost alone in his day visioned Ireland as we of today would surely have her: not free merely, but Gaelic as well; not Gaelic merely, but free as well,

In a closer spiritual communion with him now than ever before or perhaps ever again, in a spiritual communion with those of his day, living and dead, who suffered with him in English prisons, in communion of spirit too with our own dear comrades who suffer in English prisons today, and speaking on their behalf as well as our own, we pledge to Ireland our love, and we pledge to English rule in Ireland our hate. This is a place of peace, sacred to the dead, where men should speak with all charity and with all restraint; but I hold it a Christian thing, as O'Donovan Rossa held it, to hate evil, to hate untruth, to hate oppression, and, hating them, to strive to overthrow them.

Our foes are strong and wise and wary but, strong and wise and wary as they are, they cannot undo the miracles of God who ripens in the hearts of young men the seeds sown by the young men of a former generation. And the seeds sown by the young men of '65 and '67 are coming to their miraculous ripening today. Rulers and defenders of realms had need to be wary if they would guard against such processes. Life springs from death; and from the graves of patriot men and women spring living nations. The defenders of this realm have worked well in secret and in the open. They think that they have pacified Ireland. They think that they have purchased half of us and intimidated the other half. They think that they have provided against everything; but the fools, the fools, the fools! – they have left us our Fenian dead, and while Ireland holds these graves, Ireland unfree shall never be at peace.

When Pádraig Pearse asked Tom Clarke how impassioned the speech should be, Clarke replied: 'Make it hot as hell, throw discretion to the winds.'

The funeral procession of Jeremiah O'Donovan Rossa on 1 August 1915. He died in America and was given a hero's welcome on the return of his body to Ireland.

Mary MacSwiney
(1872–1942)

Mary MacSwiney was elected to the first
Dáil as the sister of Terence MacSwiney,
the lord mayor of Cork, who had died in a
British prison while on hunger strike. She was
vehemently opposed to the Treaty, regarding it
as a betrayal of those who had given their lives
for Ireland, and she made her feelings known in the Dáil chamber,
inflaming the situation, even though the main actors in the drama
were inclined towards reconciliation.

'This is a betrayal, a gross betrayal.'

Muriel Murphy MacSwiney (2nd from right) protesting against oppression
of Sinn Fein activists. 1922. The widow of nationalist hero, Terence
MacSwiney, protests for her sister-in-law, Mary MacSwiney, whose life
was threatened by her hunger strike in an Irish Free State Prison.

England Murdered My Husband
TERENCE MACSWINEY
Will Americans Permit the English
Free State to Murder
His Sister, Mary MacSwiney
PUZZ
England took
kill Terrence
How long wil
Free State tak
MARY MACSWINEY

From a speech to Dáil Éireann, 7 January 1922

I, for one, will have neither hand, act nor part in helping the Irish Free State to carry this nation of ours, this glorious nation that has been betrayed here tonight, into the British Empire – either with or without your hands up.

I maintain here now that this is the grossest act of betrayal that Ireland ever endured. I know some of you have done it from good motives; soldiers have done it to get a gun. God help them! Others, because they thought it best in some other way. I do not want to say a word that would prevent them from coming back to their Mother Republic; but I register my protest, and not one bit of help that we can give will we give them. The speech we have heard sounded very beautiful – as the late minister of finance can do it; he has played up to the gallery in this thing, but I tell you it may sound very beautiful but it will not do. Ireland stands on her republican government and that republican government cannot touch the pitch of the Free State without being fouled; and here and now I call on all true republicans; we all want to protect the public safety; it is our side that will do its best to protect the public safety. We want no such terrible troubles in the country as faction fights; we can never descend to the faction fights of former days; we have established a government, and we will have to protect it.

Therefore, let there be no misunderstanding, no soft talk, no *ráiméis* at this last moment of the betrayal of our country; no soft talk about union; you cannot unite a spiritual Irish Republic and a betrayal worse than Castlereagh's, because it was done for the Irish nation. You may talk about the will of the Irish people, as Arthur Griffith did; you know it is not the will of the Irish people; it is the fear of the Irish people, as the lord mayor of Cork says; and tomorrow or another day when they come to their senses they will talk of those who betrayed them today as they talk of Castlereagh. Make no doubt about it. This is a betrayal, a gross betrayal; and the fact that it is only a small majority, and that majority is not united; half of them look for a gun and the other half are looking for the fleshpots of the Empire. I tell you here there can be no union between the representatives of the Irish Republic and the so-called Free State.

Michael Collins
(1890–1922)

Michael Collins, a native of County Cork, became involved in radical politics, joining Sinn Féin in 1908. Although he was one of the planners of the 1916 Rising he avoided execution. He was minister for finance in the first Dáil, set up after Sinn Féin declared Ireland's independence in the wake of the 1918 general election. The war of independence that ensued ended in a truce with Britain in July 1921. Collins was part of the delegation sent to London to negotiate a treaty. It resulted in the partition of the island and, ultimately, civil war. Collins was assassinated by the anti-Treaty forces in County Cork on 22 August 1922.

*'I stand for every action,
no matter how it looked.'*

Michael Collins (Love of Ireland), 1922
(oil on canvas), by John Lavery

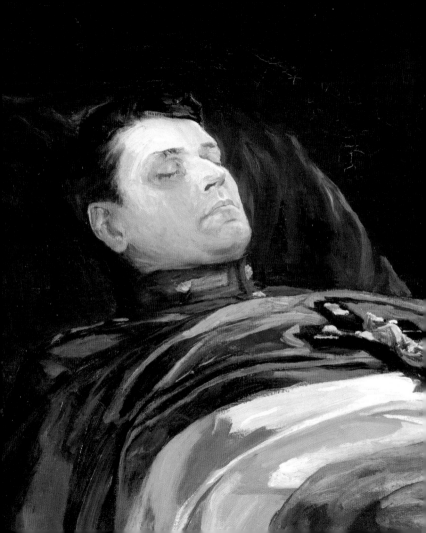

From his speech to Dáil Éireann, 19 December 1922

Much has been said in private session about the action of the plenipotentiaries in signing at all or in signing without first putting their document before the Cabinet. Now, I want to make this clear. The answer which I gave and that signature which I put on that document would have been the same in Dublin or in Berlin, or in New York or in Paris. If we had been in Dublin the difference in distance would have made this difference, that we would have been able to consult not only the members of the Cabinet but many members of the Dáil and many good friends. There has been talk about the 'atmosphere' and there has been talk about 'slippery slopes'. Such talk is beside the point. I knew the atmosphere of London of old and I knew many other things about it of old. If the members knew so much about 'slippery slopes' before we went there why did they not speak then? The slopes were surely slippery, but it is easy to be wise afterwards. I submit that such observations are entirely beside the point. And if my signature has been given in error, I stand by it whether it has or not, and I am not going to take refuge behind any kind of subterfuge. I stand up over that signature and I give the same decision at this moment in this assembly.

It has also been suggested that the delegation broke down before the first bit of English bluff. I would remind the deputy who used that expression that England put up quite a good bluff for the last five years here and I did not break down before that bluff. And does anybody think that the respect I compelled from them in a few years was in any way lowered during two months of negotiations? That also is beside the point.

The results of our labour are before the Dáil. Reject or accept.

The President has suggested that a greater result could have been obtained by more skilful handling. Perhaps so. But there again the fault rests with the Dáil. It is not afterwards the Dáil should have found out our limitations. Surely the Dáil knew it when they selected us, and our abilities could not have been expected to increase because we were chosen as plenipotentiaries by the Dáil.

The delegates have been blamed for various things. It is scarcely too much to say that they have been blamed for not returning with recognition of the Irish Republic. They are blamed, at any rate, for not having done much better. It is further suggested that by the result of their labours the delegation made a resumption of hostilities certain. That again rests with the Dáil; they should have chosen a better delegation and it was before we went to London that should have been done, not when we returned.

And as this may be the last opportunity I shall ever have of speaking publicly to the Dáil, I want to say that there was never an Irishman placed in such a position as I was by reason of these negotiations. I had got a certain name, whether I deserved it or not, and I knew when I was going over there that I was being placed in a position that I could not reconcile, and that I could not in the public mind be reconciled with they thought I stood for, no matter what we brought back – and if we brought back the recognition of the Republic – but I knew that the English would make a greater effort if I were there than they would if I were not there, and I didn't care if my popularity was sacrificed or not. I should have been unfair to my own country if I did not go there. Members of the Dáil well remember that I protested against being selected.

I only want to say that I stand for every action as an individual member of the Cabinet, which I suppose I shall be no longer; I stand for every action, no matter how it looked publicly, and I shall always like the men to remember me like that. In coming to the decision I did I tried to weigh what my own responsibility was.

Deputies have spoken about whether dead men would approve of it, and they have spoken of whether children yet unborn will approve of it, but few of them have spoken as to whether the living approve of it. In my own small way I have tried to have before my mind what the whole lot of them would think of it. And the proper way for us to look at it is in that way.

There is no man here who has more regard for the dead men than I have. I don't think it is fair to be quoting them against us. I think the decision ought to be a clear decision on the documents as they are before us – on the Treaty as it is before us. On that we shall be judged, as to whether we have done the right thing in our own conscience or not.

Don't let us put the responsibility, the individual responsibility, upon anybody else. Let us take that responsibility ourselves and let us in God's name abide by the decision.

William Butler Yeats
(1865–1939)

William Butler Yeats, Protestant nationalist, poet, playwright and Nobel laureate, was appointed to Seanad Éireann in 1922. His most memorable speech from the floor of the Senate was in 1925 on the subject of the introduction of a ban on divorce. Speaking from a Protestant perspective and always sensitive to the possibility of division between Catholics and Protestants, Yeats delivered an impassioned attack on the government, pointing out that a ban on divorce was a sectarian act that would alienate Northern Irish Protestants.

'You will put a wedge into the midst of this nation.'

Portrait of W.B. Yeats by his father, John Butler Yeats.

From his speech to Seanad Éireann, 11 June 1925

I judge from conversations that I have had with various persons that many would welcome a very simple solution, namely, that the Catholic members should remain absent when a Bill of Divorce was brought before the House that concerned Protestants and non-Catholics only, and that it would be left to the Protestant members, or some committee appointed by those Protestant members, to be dealt with. I think it would be the first instinct of the members of both Houses to adopt some such solution and it is obvious, I think, that from every point of view of national policy and national reputation that it would be a wise policy.

It is perhaps the deepest political passion with this nation that North and South be united into one nation. If it ever comes that North and South unite, the North will not give up any liberty which she already possesses under her constitution. You will then have to grant to another people what you refuse to grant to those within your borders. If you show that this country, Southern Ireland, is going to be governed by Catholic ideas and by Catholic ideas alone, you will never get the North. You will create an impassable barrier between South and North, and you will pass more and more Catholic laws, while the North will, gradually, assimilate its divorce and other laws to those of England. You will put a wedge into the midst of this nation. I do not think this House has ever made a more serious decision than the decision which, I believe, it is about to make on this question. You will not get the North if you impose on the minority what the minority consider to be oppressive legislation. I have no doubt whatever that in the next few years the minority will make it perfectly plain that it does consider it exceedingly oppressive legislation to deprive it of rights which it has held since the 17th century. These rights were won by the labours of John Milton and other great men, and won after strife, which is a famous part of the history of the Protestant people.

There is a reason why this country did not act upon what was its first impulse, and why this House and the Dáil did not act on their first impulse. Some of you may probably know that when the committee was set up to draw up the constitution of the Free State, it was urged to incorporate in the constitution the indissolubility of marriage and it refused to do so. That was the expression of the political mind of Ireland. You are now urged to act on the advice of men who do not express the political mind, but who express the religious mind. I admit it must be exceedingly difficult for members of this House to resist the pressure that has been brought upon them. In the long warfare of this country with England the Catholic clergy took the side of the people, and owing to that they possess here an influence that they do not possess anywhere else in Europe.

You are to force your theology upon persons who are not of your religion. It is not a question of finding it legally difficult or impossible to grant to a minority what the majority does not wish for itself. If you legislate upon such grounds there is no reason why you should stop there. Once you attempt legislation upon religious grounds you open the way for every kind of intolerance and for every kind of religious persecution.

I think it is tragic that within three years of this country gaining its independence we should be discussing a measure which a minority of this nation considers to be grossly oppressive. I am proud to consider myself a typical man of that minority. We against whom you have done this thing, are no petty people. We are one of the great stocks of Europe. We are the people of Burke; we are the people of Grattan; we are the people of Swift, the people of Emmet, the people of Parnell. We have created the most of the modern literature of this country. We have created the best of its political intelligence. Yet I do not altogether regret what has happened. I shall be able to find out, if not I, my children will be able to find out whether we have lost our stamina or not. You have defined our position and you have given us a popular following. If we have not lost our stamina then your victory will be brief, and your defeat final, and when it comes this nation may be transformed.

John A. Costello
(1891–1976)

In 1933, after Fianna Fáil's 1932 election victory, the Army Comrades Association (ACA) was formed to protect speakers at Cumann na nGaedheal meetings – they wore blue shirts, used fascist-style salutes and excluded non-Christians and foreigners. When De Valera banned the ACA it responded by merging with Cumann na nGaedheal to form a new party, Fine Gael, whose TDs defiantly wore the blueshirt uniform in the Oireachteas. In 1934 De Valera introduced a bill outlawing the wearing of the uniform in public. Fine Gael TD John A. Costello would later lead two coalition governments in the late 1940s and mid-1950s.

*'The general sense of the community
is being revolted by this.'*

John Costello on a visit to the United States.

From his speech to Dáil Éireann opposing the Wearing of Uniform (Restriction) Bill, 28 February 1934

There are so many reasons why deputies should vote against this bill, why every possible effort should be made to prevent it ever becoming law, that it is difficult to choose between them. I propose to take two main reasons. In the first place, this is a bill, as the minister for justice has frankly admitted – perhaps not in so many words – brought in by a political party which, for the moment forms the government, against a political party which, for the moment forms the chief opposition in this State and in this House. It is brought in against this political party by another political party, to be operated, if it ever becomes law, by a political police force. That is my first objection to this bill. My second objection is, if possible, perhaps a more fundamental objection, because it is a bill which is an invasion of individual rights and of the constitutional freedom which was guaranteed to the citizens of this state by the constitution which was brought into force on 6 December 1922. Deputies should pause before they give any support to the precedent that is set up by this bill. As I submit to the House and will show, it is an effort to prevent a lawful political movement, merely because that movement, as I mentioned on a previous occasion, menaces the political longevity of the Fianna Fáil party.

It is only one step from preventing a political party pursuing its ideas and aims by particular methods which are anti-phatic to the political party at the moment in power, to preventing a political party from functioning in a lawful way in this State merely because it is thought to be a menace to the political longevity of the political party in power. That is the real danger that lies in this bill. Even if the ministry were honest – I say and believe that they are not honest and their actions over the last 12 months have proved how dishonest they are – this is not a bill that ought to be passed by this House. No matter what they may think, the present government will not be there for all time so that another government with this precedent in front of them may use similar provisions for the purpose of stifling lawful political activity, the lawful expression of political activity in this country which was politically uneducated in 1922, which is still, in some measure, politically uneducated and can only be politically educated along proper lines by the normal development of political parties and the clash of political ideas. This bill is going to put an end to that. It is going to set a precedent for anybody who wishes to stifle for all time such portions of the right of freedom of speech and the right of free association as will be left to the citizens of this State when the present government has been put out of power.

We wear a blue shirt ... not for the purpose of creating disorder, as the minister for justice would have us believe, but for the purpose of showing their comradeship and to indicate the decent people who are present at meetings and not the rowdies who are really the cause of disturbance at public meetings.

The minister gave extracts from various laws on the continent, but he carefully refrained from drawing attention to the fact that the Blackshirts were victorious in Italy and that the Hitler Shirts were victorious in Germany, as, assuredly, in spite of this bill and in spite of the Public Safety Act, the Blueshirts will be victorious in the Irish Free State. The minister bans political emblems of all kinds, classes and descriptions. Every article, every token, every emblem of any kind that may be regarded as indicating support of a particular political party is unlawful. The present government, so far from upholding the law and bringing it into repute, is bringing it into disrepute – that is a bad thing. New crimes are being created which no single individual, beyond the front bench of the Fianna Fáil party, believes are crimes. The general sense of the community is being revolted by this, and it will tend to bring the law into disrepute instead of respect.

Sir James Craig
(1871–1940)

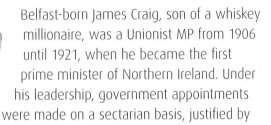

Belfast-born James Craig, son of a whiskey millionaire, was a Unionist MP from 1906 until 1921, when he became the first prime minister of Northern Ireland. Under his leadership, government appointments were made on a sectarian basis, justified by Craig, who believed that the state had to be protected from the subversion of Catholics. Despite his increasing disengagement from Westminster during his premiership, Craig was made a baronet in 1918 and in 1927 was created Viscount Craigavon of Stormont. He died in office.

*'We are a Protestant Parliament
and a Protestant State.'*

From a speech to the House of Commons of Northern Ireland, Stormont, 24 April 1934

In the South they boasted of a Catholic state. They still boast of Southern Ireland being a Catholic state.

All I boast of is that we are a Protestant Parliament and a Protestant state. It would be rather interesting for historians of the future to compare a Catholic state launched in the South with a Protestant state launched in the North and to see which gets on the better and prospers the more. It is most interesting for me at the moment to watch how they are progressing. I am doing my best always to top the bill and to be ahead of the South.

There are strong arguments why we should protect our own loyal workingmen and if any preference is given they should be given that preference over anyone coming across the border. We have a long way to go yet. I think we should take every means as early as possible to urge the public to employ only loyalists. I say only loyalists. I do not care what their religion may be. I say as long as they are loyal people we will engage them and we will give them every chance and will help them, but we must be particular to see that none of these men can burrow underneath our constitution, working day and night to destroy Ulster, which took us so long to build up.

I would ask the genial and kindly Member for South Fermanagh what hardship there will be if he uses his strong political influence to keep people in the Free State and says to them, 'You who are not able to find work stay there. Do not come into Ulster. It is the most bigoted and horribly blackmouth place on earth. Do not come in here. Stay in that glorious country, that part where it is overflowing with milk and honey, that new Jerusalem. Stay there and for God's sake do not put your noses across the border.'

Let them all find employment in their own area, and then we will have a better chance of picking up the unemployed upon the exchanges that already exist in the Ulster area. Let us be consistent in all these matters, and let us never forget another matter, and this is of very great importance in the border counties. I do not suppose from the date that Mr Redmond on the one hand and Lord Carson and myself on the other hand attended the conference at Buckingham Palace, I do not suppose from that day to this that the counties of Tyrone and Fermanagh have ever been out of my mind. They must get all the support and help they ask for. They must get all the help they require, and so far as I am concerned and my colleagues in the government are concerned it will never be refused them. Never. I do not mind going a step further and saying that the government will be ready to pass even stronger legislation if it is found necessary to prevent anything I have hinted at today happening. We will not hesitate for one moment to make safe and sure what we have there and what we intend to hold.

Éamon De Valera
(1882–1975)

De Valera was born in New York, but was brought up by his father's relatives in Ireland. He was one of the leaders of the 1916 Rising but escaped execution because of his US citizenship. He led Sinn Féin to victory in the 1918 elections and became president of the First Dáil. He resigned after the ratification of the Treaty in 1922. After the Civil War he founded Fianna Fáil, led three governments and was President of Ireland from 1959 to 1973. On St Patrick's Day 1943, the 50th anniversary of the Gaelic League, he addressed the nation, promoting Irish language and culture.

'That Ireland which we dreamed of.'

Eamon de Valera, MP for East Clare at the time this portrait was taken at A.H. Poole Photographic Studio in Waterford in 1918.

From his address on Radio Éireann, St Patrick's Day, 17 March 1943

Acutely conscious though we all are of the misery and desolation in which the greater part of the world is plunged, let us turn aside for a moment to that ideal Ireland that we would have.

That Ireland which we dreamed of would be the home of a people who valued material wealth only as the basis of right living, of a people who were satisfied with frugal comfort and devoted their leisure to the things of the spirit – a land whose countryside would be bright with cosy homesteads – whose fields and villages would be joyous with the sounds of industry, with the romping of sturdy children, the contests of athletic youths and the laughter of comely maidens, whose firesides would be forums for the wisdom of serene old age. It would, in a word, be the home of a people living the life that God desires that man should live.

With the tidings that make such an Ireland possible, St Patrick came to our ancestors 1500 years ago, promising happiness here as well as happiness hereafter. It was the pursuit of such an Ireland that later made our country worthy to be called the Island of

Saints and Scholars. It was the idea of such an Ireland, happy, vigorous, spiritual, that fired the imagination of our poets, that made successive generations of patriotic men give their lives to win religious and political liberty, and that will urge men in our own and future generations to die, if need be, so that these liberties may be preserved.

One hundred years ago the Young Irelanders, by holding up the vision of such an Ireland before the people, inspired our nation and moved it spiritually as it had hardly been moved since the golden age of Irish civilisation. Fifty years after the Young Irelanders, the founders of the Gaelic League similarly inspired and moved the people of their day, as did later the leaders of the Volunteers. We of this time, if we have the will and the active enthusiasm, have the opportunity to inspire and move our generation in like manner. We can do so by keeping this thought of a noble future for our country constantly before our minds, ever seeking in action to bring that future into being, and ever remembering that it is to our nation as a whole that that future must apply.

For many, the pursuit of the material is a necessity. Man, to express himself fully and to make the best use of the talents God has given him, needs a certain minimum of comfort and leisure. A section of our people have not yet this minimum. They rightly strive to secure it, and it must be our aim and the aim of all who are just and wise to assist the effort. But many have got more than is required and are free, if they choose, to devote themselves more completely to cultivating the things of the mind, and in particular those which mark us out as a distinct nation.

The first of these latter is the national language. It is for us what no other language can be. It is our very own. It is more than a symbol; it is an essential part of our nationhood. It has been moulded by the thought of a hundred generations of our forebears. As a vehicle of 3000 years of our history, the language is for us precious beyond measure. To part with it would be to abandon a great part of ourselves, to lose the key of our past, to cut away the roots from the tree. With the language gone we could never aspire again to being more than half a nation.

For my part, I believe that this outstanding mark of our nationhood can be preserved and made forever safe by this generation. I am indeed certain of it, but I know that it cannot be saved without understanding and co-operation and effort and sacrifice. The task of restoring the language as the everyday speech of our people is a task as great as any nation ever undertook. But it is a noble task. As long as the language lives on the lips of the people as their natural speech in any substantial part of this land we are assured of success if – if we are in earnest.

Bail ó Dhia oraibh agus bail go gcuire Sé ar an obair atá romhainn. Go gcúmhdaí Dia sinn agus gur fiú sinn choíche, mar náisiún, na tiolacaí a thug Pádraig chugainn. Go dtuga an tUilechumachtach, A thug slán go dtí seo ón anachain is ón mí-ádh atá ar oiread sin náisiún eile de bharr an chogaidh seo, scáth agus didean dúinn go dtí an deireadh, agus go ndeonaí Sé gur fiú sinn cion uasal a dhéanamh sa saol nua atá romhainn.

[God bless you and bless the work that lies before us. May God protect us, and may we always, as a nation, be worthy of the gifts that St Patrick brought us. May the Almighty, Who has brought us safe until now from the calamity and misfortune that have befallen so many other nations in consequence of this war, grant us shelter and protection to the end and make us worthy to play a noble part in the new world of the future.]

Éamon De Valera

When the Second World War ended in May 1945, British Prime Minister Winston Churchill spoke on the BBC on the occasion of the fifth anniversary of his premiership and used the opportunity to attack Ireland's stance of neutrality during the conflict. De Valera responded on Irish radio a few days later, making a clear and forceful case for the position taken by Ireland.

> *'There are some things which
> it is my duty to say.'*

From his address on Radio Éireann in response to Churchill's broadcast, 16 May 1945

Certain newspapers have been very persistent in looking for my answer to Mr Churchill's recent broadcast. I know the kind of answer I am expected to make. I know the reply I would have given a quarter of a century ago. But I have deliberately decided that that is not the reply I shall make tonight. I shall strive not to be guilty of adding any fuel to the flames of hatred and passion which, if continued to be fed, promise to burn up whatever is left by the war of decent human feeling in Europe.

Mr Churchill makes it clear that, in certain circumstances, he would have violated our neutrality and that he would justify his action by Britain's necessity. It seems strange to me that Mr Churchill does not see that this, if accepted, would mean that Britain's necessity became a moral code and that when this necessity became sufficiently great, other people's rights were not to count.

It is quite true that other great powers believe in this same code – in their own regard – and have behaved in accordance with it. That is precisely why we have the disastrous succession of wars – World War no. 1 and World War no. 2 – and shall it be World War no. 3?

Surely Mr Churchill must see that, if his contention be admitted in our regard, a like justification can be framed for similar acts of aggression elsewhere and no small nation adjoining a great power could ever hope to be permitted to go its own way in peace.

It is, indeed, fortunate that Britain's necessity did not reach the point when Mr Churchill would have acted. All credit to him that he successfully resisted the temptation which, I have no doubt, many times assailed him in his difficulties and to which I freely admit many leaders might have easily succumbed. It is, indeed, hard for the strong to be just to the weak, but acting justly always has its rewards.

By resisting his temptation in this instance, Mr Churchill, instead of adding another horrid chapter to the already bloodstained record of the relations between England and this country, has advanced the cause of international morality an important step.

That Mr Churchill should be irritated when our neutrality stood in the way of what he thought he vitally needed, I understand, but that he or any thinking person in Britain or elsewhere should fail to see the reason for our neutrality, I find it hard to conceive.

Suppose Germany had won the war, had invaded and occupied England, and that after a long lapse of time and many bitter struggles she was finally brought to acquiesce in admitting England's right to freedom, and let England go, but not the whole of England, all but, let us say, the six southern counties … commanding the entrance to the narrow seas.

Let us suppose, further, that after all this had happened Germany was engaged in a great war in which she could show that she was on the side of the freedom of a number of small nations. Would Mr Churchill as an Englishman who believed that his own nation had as good a right to freedom as any other – not freedom for a part merely, but freedom for the whole – would he, whilst Germany still maintained the partition of his country and occupied six counties of it, would he lead his partitioned England to join with Germany in a crusade? I do not think Mr Churchill would.

Would he think the people of partitioned England an object of shame if they stood neutral in such circumstances? I do not think Mr Churchill would.

Mr Churchill is proud of Britain's stand alone, after France had fallen and before America entered the war.

Could he not find in his heart the generosity to acknowledge that there is a small nation that stood alone, not for one year or two, but for several hundred years against aggression; that endured spoliations, famines, massacres in endless succession; that was clubbed many times into insensibility, but that each time, on returning consciousness, took up the fight anew; a small nation that could never be got to accept defeat and has never surrendered her soul?

Mr Churchill is justly proud of his nation's perseverance against heavy odds. But we in this island are still prouder of our people's perseverance for freedom through all the centuries. We have pledged ourselves to the dead generations who have preserved intact for us this glorious heritage, that we too will strive to be faithful to the end, and pass on this tradition unblemished.

In latter years I have had a vision of a nobler and better ending, better for both our peoples and the future of mankind. For that I have now been long working. I regret that it is not to this nobler purpose that Mr Churchill is lending his hand rather than by the abuse of a people who have done him no wrong, trying to find in a crisis like the present excuse for continuing the injustice of the mutilation of our country.

Noël Browne
(1915–1997)

Noël Browne, a medical doctor specialising in the treatment of TB, was elected to the Dáil in 1948 and was appointed minister for health. The previous year health legislation had been enacted providing for free ante- and post-natal health care and free health care for under 16s. Browne was asked to implement the scheme but was opposed by the doctors' lobby, who felt their earning power would be reduced, and by the Catholic hierarchy, who were concerned that socialism was creeping in through a back door. Unsupported by the Cabinet, Browne was unable to implement the scheme. He resigned in 1951, handing the correspondence on the issue to *The Irish Times*, sparking the notorious 'Mother and Child' crisis.

'I know the consequences which may follow my action.'

From his Resignation speech to Dáil Éireann, 12 April 1951

I have pledged myself to introduce a mother and child health scheme which would not embody a means test. Since I could not succeed in fulfilling my promise in this regard I consider it my duty to vacate my office.

While I as a Catholic accept unequivocally and unreservedly the views of the hierarchy on this matter, I have not been able to accept the manner in which this matter has been dealt with my former colleagues in the government.

In June 1948, the government authorised me to introduce a mother and child health scheme to provide free maternity treatment and free treatment for children up to the age of 16. On 10 October 1950, I was informed that His Grace the Archbishop of Dublin wished to see me in connection with the scheme. I was informed that at a meeting of the hierarchy His Grace and Their Lordships [the Bishops of Ferns and Galway] had been appointed to put before the government certain objections which the hierarchy saw in the scheme; that I was being informed of these as a matter of courtesy before transmission to the taoiseach as head of the government.

About the 9th or 10th of November I learned that the taoiseach had received a letter, dated 10 October 1950, from the Bishop of Ferns, as secretary to the hierarchy. The taoiseach gave me this letter for my observations with a view to a reply. The objections in the letter appeared to be those read to me by His Grace the Archbishop of Dublin, during my interview on 11 October, and, in the light of the later events, I concluded that it had been transmitted solely for the purpose of record and formal reply. I, therefore, acting on this assumption, prepared a draft letter for transmission by the taoiseach to His Lordship of Ferns in reply to the various points raised in their letter. In this answer I substantially recapitulated the case I had made when I met His Grace and Their Lordships at Drumcondra on 11 October. I would like to emphasise that, as I still believed that His Grace and Their Lordships had been reassured by the case made by me on 11 October, I merely regarded this reply also as being for purposes of record by the hierarchy. I sent this draft to the taoiseach shortly after mid-November to be forwarded by him to the hierarchy. As I heard nothing further about the matter from either the hierarchy or the taoiseach until a couple of weeks ago I had no reason to believe that the hierarchy were not fully satisfied, and the work of preparing for the introduction of the mother and child scheme continued, and on 6 March its early implementation was widely publicised by me.

On 9 March I received a letter from His Grace the Archbishop of Dublin. I was surprised to hear that His Grace might not approve of the scheme, and declared that the objections which had been raised by him in October had not been resolved. Following receipt of His Grace's letter, a copy of which was sent by His Grace to the taoiseach, the latter suggested to me on 15 March that I should take steps at once to consult the hierarchy regarding their objections to the scheme. I then learned to my distress and amazement that the reply to their Lordships' letter which I had prepared and sent to the taoiseach in the previous November had, in fact, never been sent by him.

I pointed out that his failure to send this letter had the effect that I remained under the erroneous impression that the objections of the hierarchy had been fully resolved and that I could proceed with the scheme. I was surprised also to learn from the taoiseach that he had been in constant communication with His Grace the Archbishop of Dublin on this matter since the receipt of the letter of 10 October from the hierarchy, so presumably he was fully aware that their Lordships' objections were still unresolved.

The letter sent by the taoiseach on 27 March 1951, to the Bishop of Ferns, enclosing my observations, refers to the scheme 'advocated by the minister for health', thereby implying that the scheme was not advocated or supported by himself or other members of the government. In a letter of 5 April from His Grace the Archbishop of Dublin it is stated that [the hierarchy] were pleased to note that no evidence had been supplied that the proposed mother and child scheme advocated by the minister of health enjoys the support of the government.

It is a fact noted by many people that in no public speeches did ministers of the government other than myself speak in favour of this measure. I regret that for the want of courage on their part they should have allowed the scheme to progress so very far – that they should have failed to keep me informed of the true position in regard to their own attitude and the attitude of others. I have, consequently, been allowed by their silence to commit myself to the country to implement a scheme which certain members of the government at least did not want, on their own admission, to see implemented and which they were in fact aware could not be implemented.

I trust that the standards manifested in these dealings are not customary in the public life of this or any other democratic nation and I hope that my experience has been exceptional.

I have not lightly decided to take the course I have taken. I know the consequences which may follow my action. The honesty of my motives will be attacked by able men; my aims will be called in question; ridicule and doubt will be cast upon the wisdom of my insistence in striving to realise the declared objectives of the party to which I belonged.

I lay down my seal of office content that you, and the people who are our masters here, shall judge whether I have striven to honour the trust placed in me.

Portrait of Noël Browne by Robert Ballagh, in the National Gallery of Ireland.

Seán Lemass
(1889–1971)

In 1916 Dubliner Seán Lemass was one of the youngest men to take part in the Rising. He took the anti-Treaty side in the Civil War and joined with De Valera in founding Fianna Fáil, holding the government portfolio for industry and commerce in the 1930s. He became taoiseach in 1959. In the 1950s Ireland wasn't thriving, failing to produce the increase in living standards and opportunities being enjoyed all over Europe. Fianna Fáil had lost the 1954 general election and Lemass came up with an ambitious economic plan, promising to create 100,000 jobs within five years.

> *'The effort needed is not beyond the country's capabilities.'*

Taoiseach Seán Lemass.

From his speech to a Fianna Fáil party meeting, Clery's ballroom, Dublin, 11 October 1955

The FF party has accepted the conclusion that the economic development programme which it initiated 25 years ago has not proved to be sufficient to bring about all the economic and social progress which we desired and believe can be accomplished.

We have used this present period of release from immediate responsibility for government in reviewing our programme and preparing new plans so that under FF leadership, the nation can experience another era of advancement. The proposals which I am about to outline are based on the view that the successful application of a sound development policy requires an adequate and carefully prepared investment programme. We do not believe, however, that Irish progress and prosperity can be secured by government action alone, and an essential part of the proposals are therefore concerned with the promotion of a sufficient and expanding volume of investment on private account.

The aims of the proposals are, firstly, to give the national economy the necessary initial boost; secondly, to bring about an increase in private investment activity to the extent required to secure an adequate and continuing expansion of the scope and efficiency of private productive enterprise; and thirdly, to show that the effort needed is not beyond the country's possibilities.

The main proposal is that as a first step to the attainment of full employment, the government should undertake a positive spending programme spread over a five-year period. This should be financed otherwise than by taxation or by borrowing from current savings and planned on a scale estimated to be sufficient, taking into account the volume of private activity, to raise total national outlay to a level calculated to be adequate to set up a demand for the whole of the labour available for employment. Our view is that the government must carry the main burden in the first instance, but must so arrange its programme that it can gradually fade out of the picture, leaving private economic activity the main basis of national prosperity.

It is clear that the scale of the public expenditure which will be required to bring national outlay to full employment level within five years will be very considerable. FF rejects the view that the sole object of government policy should be to keep public expenditure at the lowest possible level. The primary aims of FF's policy have been in the past, and will always be, to increase the nation's wealth and to improve the living conditions of the people. These aims over-ride other considerations.

On the average during the year, 8.1 per cent of workers were unemployed. Since 1946, the total labour force has declined by 61,000, that is at an annual rate of over 7500 persons or 0.6 per cent per annum. Net emigration averages about 25,000 per year of which from one half to two thirds may be assumed to be preventable in the sense that a fair prospect of security of employment in Ireland would keep that number from emigrating.

It is safe to assume, however, that an increase over five years in the number of jobs by 100,000 or an average rate of increase of 20,000 per year would result in full employment as ordinarily understood and the end of abnormal emigration. At the end of five years, 15,000 new jobs per annum should enable full employment to be maintained.

The proposals which I have outlined can do no more than ensure that the efforts of the Irish people to improve their living conditions, to end unemployment and to reduce emigration will be facilitated by a proper disposal of national resources and not impeded by their partial immobilisation as at present.

They are put forward in the belief that this country's inability to achieve the same employment conditions and living standards as other small west European countries is due solely to the circumstances which have prevented the full utilisation of available resources and not to any incapacity of the Irish people to accomplish the same productive effort as these other countries have achieved.

It is along these lines that FF is planning the nation's future progress. In the present task of completing these plans and the ultimate task of fulfilling them, FF asks the cooperation and support of all sections of the Irish people.

Supporters carrying Seán Lemass after his success in a Dublin by-election on 12 March 1924. Lemass was a member of Anti-Treaty Sinn Féin and a founding member of the Fianna Fáil party in 1926.

Frank Aiken

(1898–1983)

Frank Aiken was born in County Armagh and was a teenage recruit to the Irish Volunteers. He fought in the War of Independence and took the anti-Treaty side in the Civil War, but was quick to issue a ceasefire after taking over as commander-in-chief of the IRA. He was minister for finance in the first Fianna Fáil government in 1932, and was minister for defence during the Second World War, a difficult role in a neutral nation. He was fearful of the possibilities of the general proliferation of nuclear weapons and, as minister for external affairs in the 1950s and 1960s, he made strong representations to the UN on the subject.

'Portable weapons which are the monopoly of the great powers today become the weapons of smaller powers and revolutionary groups tomorrow.'

Photograph of Frank Aiken sitting at his desk as minister for external affairs.

From his speech to the UN General Assembly on the Irish Non-Proliferation Treaty, 17 October 1958

An important factor in this changing world situation today is the imminent danger that more and more states will come to possess nuclear weapons.

With this in mind we have submitted certain amendments to the draft resolution of the 17 powers. We have also tabled a draft resolution.

The amendments and the resolution are in the hands of the committee. The amendments, if accepted, would urge the non-nuclear powers, during a specified period, to refrain from manufacturing or acquiring nuclear weapons and would urge the nuclear powers to refrain from supplying such weapons to states which do not now possess them. We regard the proposed temporary measure of nuclear restriction as only a step towards a permanent ban on the further dissemination of nuclear weapons – permanent in the sense that it should remain in being until the total abolition of nuclear weapons renders it superfluous. Similarly in the case of our draft resolution, which proposes an ad hoc commission to study the problem of the dissemination of nuclear weapons, it is our hope and belief that this study would lead to a permanent ban on such dissemination. Both our amendments and our draft resolution, therefore, are conceived as steps towards the restriction of nuclear weapons – a restriction which in its turn would be a step towards their abolition.

The first point I wish to stress, Mr Chairman, is that as this committee, and the great powers represented in it, are unable speedily to abolish nuclear weapons completely, they ought at least, in our opinion, to take steps aimed at preventing the threat from becoming even greater. It is, in our opinion, a great tragedy that the Baruch proposals for the international control of nuclear weapons and nuclear development were not accepted and implemented 12 years ago. If we do not soon succeed in limiting the number of states making or possessing nuclear weapons, the problem of saving the world from nuclear destruction may well have passed beyond the power of man to solve long before another 12 years have passed.

The danger of nuclear weapons to humanity, it seems to us, does not merely increase in direct ratio to the number of those possessing them. It seems likely to increase in geometric progression. Those who now possess nuclear weapons are a few great and highly developed states, with great urban populations, with much to lose and little to gain in a nuclear war. Their potential adversaries are in the same case and have the power to retaliate. As in the case of every other military invention, however, the harnessing of nuclear energy for military purposes is bound to become simpler and cheaper with the passing of time. Sooner or later, therefore, unless this organisation takes urgent preventive steps, this weapon will pass into the hands of states with much less to lose. Furthermore, as it comes into their hands, it may give them a temporary but enormous advantage over their adversaries – an advantage which they will be sorely tempted to exploit.

We can all think, Mr Chairman, of several regions of the world where fierce antagonisms exist, held in suspense only by a kind of truce or deadlock. That truce, that deadlock, could be broken all too easily if one side or the other possessed nuclear weapons. In short, the nuclear stalemate ceases to apply once nuclear weapons begin to come into the hands of smaller countries. Furthermore, nothing except international measures to prevent the dissemination of such weapons can prevent them from coming, ultimately, not merely to small and poor states but also to revolutionary organisations. All through history portable weapons which are the monopoly of the great powers today become the weapons of smaller powers and revolutionary groups tomorrow. And since local wars and revolutions almost always involve some degree of great power patronage and rivalry, the use of nuclear weapons by a small state or revolutionary group could lead, only too easily, to the outbreak of general war. One obsolete, Hiroshima-type bomb, used by a small and desperate country to settle a local quarrel, could be the detonator for worldwide thermonuclear war, involving the destruction of our whole civilisation.

Photograph of members of the Cabinet, including Eamon de Valera, Seán Lemass, and Frank Aiken.

John F. Kennedy
(1917–1963)

John F. Kennedy is famous as the first Irish Catholic US president and for his assassination in 1963. Earlier that year he visited Ireland, a much publicised event that has been written into the annals of Irish history. Ireland was pulling itself out of its economic doldrums at the time, promoting industrialisation and modernisation, and it was hoped that the president would provide a boost for the hoped-for 'economic miracle'. Kennedy, however, focused his oratory on the unique relationship between the two nations, concentrating on the independent spirit of the people and the folksy, bucolic image of the nation that appealed so much to Americans.

'Our two nations, divided by distance, have been united by history.'

From his speech to the joint houses of the Oireachtas, 28 June 1963

I am proud to be the first American president to visit Ireland during his term of office, proud to be addressing this distinguished assembly, and proud of the welcome you have given me. My presence and your welcome, however, only symbolise the many and the enduring links which have bound the Irish and the Americans since the earliest days.

Benjamin Franklin, the envoy of the American Revolution, was received by the Irish Parliament in 1772. It was neither independent nor free from discrimination at the time, but Franklin reported its members 'disposed to be friends of America'.

Our interests have been joined ever since. Franklin sent leaflets to Irish freedom fighters. O'Connell was influenced by Washington, and Emmet influenced Lincoln. Irish volunteers played so predominant a role in the American Army that Lord Mountjoy lamented in the British Parliament, 'We have lost America through the Irish.'

And so it is that our two nations, divided by distance, have been united by history. No people ever believed more deeply in the cause of

Irish freedom than the people of the United States. And no country contributed more to building my own than your sons and daughters. They came to our shores in a mixture of hope and agony, and left behind hearts, fields and a nation yearning to be free.

But today this is no longer the country of hunger and famine that those immigrants left behind. It is not rich and its progress is not yet complete, but it is, according to statistics, one of the best-fed countries in the world. Nor is it any longer a country of persecution, political or religious. It is a free country, and that is why any American feels at home.

There are those who regard this history of past strife and exile as better forgotten, but to use the phrase of Yeats, 'Let us not casually reduce that great past to a trouble of fools, for we need not feel the bitterness of the past to discover its meaning for the present and the future.'

And it is the present and the future of Ireland that today hold so much promise to my nation as well as to yours, and, indeed, to all mankind, for the Ireland of 1963, one of the youngest of nations, and the oldest of civilisations, has discovered that the achievement of nationhood is not an end, but a beginning. In the years since independence, you have undergone a new and peaceful revolution, an economic and industrial revolution, transforming the face of this land, while still holding to the old spiritual and cultural values. You have modernised your economy, harnessed your rivers, diversified your industry, liberalised your trade, electrified your farms, accelerated your rate of growth, and improved the living standard of your people.

This revolution is not yet over, nor will it be, I am sure, until a fully modern Irish economy fully shares in world prosperity. But prosperity is not enough.

One hundred and eighty-three years ago, Henry Grattan, demanding the more independent Irish Parliament that would always bear his name, denounced those who were satisfied merely by new grants of economic opportunity. 'A country,' he said, 'enlightened as Ireland, chartered as Ireland, armed as Ireland, and injured as Ireland, will not be satisfied with anything less than liberty.' And today, I am certain, free Ireland, a full fledged member of the world community, where some are not yet free, and where some counsel an acceptance of tyranny – free Ireland will not be satisfied with anything less than liberty.

I am glad, therefore, that Ireland is moving in the mainstream of current world events. For I sincerely believe that your future is as promising as your past is proud, and that your destiny lies not as a peaceful island in a sea of troubles, but as a maker and shaper of world peace. No larger nation did more to spark the cause of American independence, and independence, indeed, around the world. And no larger nation has ever provided the world with more literary and artistic genius.

This is an extraordinary country. George Bernard Shaw, speaking as an Irishman, summed up an approach to life. 'Other people,' he said, 'see things and say, "Why?" … But I dream things that never were – and I say, "Why not?"' It is that quality of the Irish, the remarkable combination of hope, confidence and imagination, that is needed more than ever today. We need men who can dream of things that never were, and ask why not. It matters not how small a nation is that seeks world peace and freedom, for, to paraphrase a citizen of my country, 'The humblest nation of all the world, when clad in the armour of a righteous cause, is stronger than all the hosts of error.'

Ireland is clad in the cause of national and human liberty with peace. To the extent that the peace is disturbed by conflict between the former colonial powers and the new and developing nations, Ireland's role is unique. For every new nation knows that Ireland was the first of the small nations in the 20th century to win its struggle for independence, and that the Irish have traditionally sent their doctors and technicians and priests to help other lands to keep their liberty alive.

The major forum for your nation's greater role in world affairs is that of protector of the weak and the voice of the small, the United Nations. In a sense, this export of talent is in keeping with an historic

Irish role. But you no longer go as exiles and emigrants but for the service of your country and, indeed, of all men. Like the Irish missionaries of medieval days, like the Wild Geese after the Battle of the Boyne, you are not content to sit by your fireside while others need your help. Nor are you content with the recollections of the past when you face the responsibilities of the present.

Great powers have their responsibilities and their burdens, but the smaller nations of the world must fulfil their obligations as well. A great Irish poet once wrote, 'I believe profoundly in the future of Ireland, that this is an isle of destiny, that that destiny will be glorious, and that when our hour has come we will have something to give to the world.'

My friends, Ireland's hour has come. You have something to give to the world, and that is a future of peace with freedom. Thank you.

Terence O'Neill
(1914–1990)

Londoner Terence O'Neill was elected to Stormont as a Unionist MP in 1946 and became the fourth prime minister of Northern Ireland in 1963. He met Taoiseach Seán Lemass at a summit in Stormont in 1965, the first time a Northern Irish prime minister had met a head of the Dublin government. Cross-border cooperation increased, particularly in the promotion of tourism and the supply of electricity. In 1968 O'Neill unveiled a programme of reforms in Northern Ireland that aimed to streamline the economy. The civil rights marches of the late 1960s provoked a violent reaction and, in a broadcast to the people of Northern Ireland, O'Neill warned that 'Northern Ireland stands at the crossroads'. The sectarian violence escalated and he resigned in April 1969.

'What kind of Ulster do you want?'

From a national television broadcast, 9 December 1968

Ulster stands at the crossroads. I believe you know me well enough by now to appreciate that I am not a man given to extravagant language. But I must say to you this evening that our conduct over the coming days and weeks will decide our future.

And now I want to say a word directly to those who have been demonstrating for civil rights. The changes which we have announced are genuine and far-reaching changes and the government as a whole is committed to them. I would not continue to preside over an administration which would water them down or make them meaningless. You will see when the members of the Londonderry Commission are appointed that we intend to live up to our words that this will be a body to command confidence and respect. You will see that legislation to appoint an ombudsman will be swiftly introduced. Perhaps you are not entirely satisfied: but this is a democracy and I ask you now with all sincerity to call your people off the streets and allow an atmosphere of change to develop. You are Ulstermen yourselves. You know we are all of us stubborn people who will not be pushed too far. I believe that most of you want change, not revolution. Your voice has been heard, and clearly heard. Your duty now is to play your part in taking the heat out of the situation before blood is shed.

But I have a word, too, for all those others who see in change a threat to our position in the United Kingdom. I say to them, unionism, armed with justice, will be a stronger cause than unionism armed merely with strength. The bully-boy tactics we saw in Armagh are no answer to these grave problems: but they incur for us the contempt of Britain and the world. And such contempt is the greatest threat to Ulster. Let the government govern and the police take care of law and order.

What are these changes which we have decided must come? They all amount to this: that in every aspect of our life justice must not only be done but be seen to be done to all sections of the community. There must be evident fairness as between one man and another.

The adoption of such reforms will not, I believe, lose a single seat for those who support the unionist cause and, indeed, some may be gained. And remember that it is with Stormont that the power of decision rests for maintaining our constitution.

And now a further word to you all. What kind of Ulster do you want? A happy and respected province in good standing with the rest of the United Kingdom? Or a place continually torn apart by riots and demonstrations and regarded by the rest of Britain as a political outcast? As always, in a democracy, the choice is yours. I will accept whatever your verdict may be. If it is your decision that we should live up to the words 'Ulster is British', which is part of our creed, then my services will be at your disposal to do what I can. But if you should want a separate inward-looking, selfish and divided Ulster, then you must seek for others to lead you along that road for I cannot and will not do it. Please weigh well all that is at stake and make your voice heard in whatever way you think best so that we may know the views not of the few, but of the many. For this is truly a time of decision and in your silence all that we have built up could be lost. I pray that you will reflect carefully and decide wisely. And I ask all our Christian people, whatever their denomination, to attend their places of worship on Sunday next to pray for the peace and harmony of our country.

Bernadette Devlin
(b. 1947)

Bernadette Devlin, a Catholic from Cookstown, County Tyrone, was a prominent campaigner in the civil rights movement of the 1960s. Elected to Parliament in 1969, she took her seat at the age of 21, the youngest woman ever elected to Westminster before the Scottish Party's Mhairi Black took the honour at the age of 20 in 2015. Her maiden speech, on her first day in the House of Commons, gave an insight into her future political career, and was described as 'electrifying' by Conservative MP Sir Norman St John Stevas.

'There is no place in society for us, the ordinary "peasants" of Northern Ireland.'

Bernadette Devlin on the campaign trail.

From her maiden speech to the House of Commons, Westminster, 22 April 1969

I understand that in making my maiden speech on the day of my arrival in Parliament and in making it on a controversial issue I flaunt [sic] the unwritten traditions of the House, but I think that the situation of my people merits the flaunting [sic] of such traditions.

As the hon. Member for Londonderry rightly said, there never was born an Englishman who understands the Irish people. Thus a man who is alien to the ordinary working Irish people cannot understand them, and I therefore respectfully suggest that the hon. gentleman has no understanding of my people, because Catholics and Protestants are the ordinary people, the oppressed people from whom I come and whom I represent. I stand here as the youngest woman in Parliament in the same tradition as the first woman ever to be elected to this Parliament, Constance Markievicz, who was elected on behalf of the Irish people.

The hon. Member for Londonderry said that he stood in Bogside. I wonder whether he could name the streets through which he walked in Bogside so that we might establish just how well acquainted he became with the area. I had never hoped to see the day when I might agree with someone who represents the bigoted and sectarian Unionist Party, which uses a deliberate policy of dividing the people in order to keep the ruling minority in power and to keep the oppressed people of Ulster oppressed. I never thought I could see the day when I should agree with any phrase uttered by the representative of such a party, but the hon. gentleman summed up the situation 'to a t'. He referred to stark, human misery. That is what I saw in Bogside. It has been there for 50 years – and that same stark human misery is to be found in the Protestant Fountain area, which the hon. gentleman would claim to represent.

These are the people the hon. gentleman would claim to want to join society. Because they are equally poverty stricken they are equally excluded from the society which the Unionist Party represents as the society of landlords who, by ancient charter of Charles II, still hold the right of the ordinary people of Northern Ireland over such things as fishing and as paying the most ridiculous and exorbitant rents, although families have lived for generations on their land. But this is the ruling minority of landlords who, for generations, have claimed to represent one section of the people and, in order to maintain their claim, divide the people into two sections and stand up in this House to say that there are those who do not wish to join society.

The people in my country who do not wish to join the society which is represented by the hon. Member for Londonderry are by far the majority. There is no place in society for us, the ordinary 'peasants' of Northern Ireland. There is no place for us in the society of landlords because we are the 'have-nots' and they are the 'haves'.

We came to the situation in Derry when the people had had enough. Since 5 October, it has been the unashamed and deliberate policy of the Unionist government to try to force an image on the civil rights movement that it was nothing more than a Catholic uprising. The people in the movement have struggled desperately to overcome that image, but it is impossible when the ruling minority are the government and control not only political matters but the so-called impartial forces of law and order. It is impossible then for us to state quite fairly where we stand.

How can we say that we are a non-sectarian movement and are for the rights of both Catholics and Protestants when, clearly, we are beaten into the Catholic areas? Never have we been beaten into the Protestant areas. When the students marched from Belfast to Derry, there was a predominant number of Protestants. The number of non-Catholics was greater than the number of Catholics. Nevertheless, we were still beaten into the Catholic area because it was in the interests of the minority and the Unionist Party to establish that we were nothing more than the Catholic uprising.

Jack Lynch
(1917–1999)

The Cork hurling and football champion was first elected to the Dáil in 1948 as a Fianna Fáil TD. In 1966 he became leader of the party, serving as taoiseach from 1966–73 and 1977–79. Violent riots and confrontation in Derry in the summer of 1969 shocked the nation. Jack Lynch made an appearance on RTÉ television on 13 August to express the country's solidarity with Northern Catholics, some of whom were by then under siege. His expression of support was interpreted as a threat to Protestants, who brought the violence onto the streets of Belfast. British troops were brought in, which calmed the situation, but only temporarily.

'The present situation cannot be allowed to contine.'

From his broadcast on RTÉ television in response to the escalation of violence in Northern Ireland, 13 August 1969

It is with deep sadness that you, Irish men and women of goodwill, and I have learned of the tragic events which have been taking place in Derry and elsewhere in the North in recent days. Irishmen in every part of this island have made known their concern at these events. This concern is heightened by the realisation that the spirit of reform and inter-communal co-operation has given way to the forces of sectarianism and prejudice. All people of goodwill must feel saddened and disappointed at this backward turn in events and must be apprehensive for the future.

The government fully share these feelings and I wish to repeat that we deplore sectarianism and intolerance in all their forms wherever they occur. The government have been very patient and have acted with great restraint over several months past. While we made our views known to the British government on a number of occasions, both by direct contact and through our diplomatic representatives in London, we were careful to do nothing that would exacerbate the situation. But it is clear now that the present situation cannot be allowed to continue.

It is evident, also, that the Stormont government is no longer in control of the situation. Indeed the present situation is the inevitable outcome of the policies pursued for decades by successive Stormont governments. It is clear, also, that the Irish government can no longer stand by and see innocent people injured and perhaps worse.

It is obvious that the RUC is no longer accepted as an impartial police force. Neither would the employment of British troops be acceptable nor would they be likely to restore peaceful conditions, certainly not in the long term. The Irish government have, therefore, requested the British government to apply immediately to the United Nations for the urgent dispatch of a peace-keeping force to the six counties of Northern Ireland and have instructed the Irish permanent secretary to the United Nations to inform the secretary-general of this request. We have also asked the British government to see to it that police attacks on the people of Derry should cease immediately.

Very many people have been injured and some of them seriously. We know that many of these do not wish to be treated in six-county hospitals. We have, therefore, directed the Irish Army authorities to have field hospitals established in County Donegal adjacent to Derry and at other points along the border where they may be necessary.

Recognising, however, that the reunification of the national territory can provide the only permanent solution for the problem, it is our intention to request the British government to enter into early negotiations with the Irish government to review the present constitutional position of the six counties of Northern Ireland.

These measures which I have outlined to you seem to the government to be those most immediately and urgently necessary.

All men and women of goodwill will hope and pray that the present deplorable and distressing situation will not further deteriorate but that it will soon be ended firstly by the granting of full equality of citizenship to every man and woman in the six-county area regardless of class, creed or political persuasion and, eventually, by the restoration of the historic unity of our country.

Pope John Paul II
(1920–2005)

Pope John Paul II was born Karol Józef Wojtyla in Wadowice, Poland, in 1920. He was ordained priest in 1946 and became the archbishop of Krakow in 1964. He was a participant in the Second Vatican Council, convened in 1962. In 1967 Pope Paul VI made him a cardinal and in 1978 he was elected pope, the first non-Italian in over 400 years. A conservative on private morality he was a strong supporter of human rights and is given credit for the fall of communism in his native Poland. He died in Italy in 2005 and was declared a saint in 2014. In 1979 he became the first pope to visit Ireland and drew enormous crowds.

'Young people of Ireland, I love you!'

From his address in Galway, 30 September 1979

*A*aos óg na hÉireann, go mbeannaí Dia dhaoibh. Dear young people, brothers and sisters of our Lord Jesus Christ, when I look at you, I see the Ireland of the future. Tomorrow, you will be the living force of your country; you will decide what Ireland will be. Tomorrow, as technicians or teachers, nurses or secretaries, farmers or tradesmen, doctors or engineers, priests or religious – tomorrow you will have the power to make dreams come true. Tomorrow, Ireland will depend on you.

When I look at you I see the future of the Church. God has his plan for the Church in Ireland, but he needs you to carry it out. What the Church will be in the future depends on your free cooperation with God's grace.

When I look at the thousands of young people here before me, I also see the challenges that you face. You carry in your hearts the rich heritage that you have received from your parents, your teachers and your priests. You carry in your hearts the treasures which Irish history and culture have given you, but you also share in the problems that Ireland faces.

The religious and moral traditions of Ireland, the very soul of Ireland, will be challenged by the temptations that spare no society in our age. Like so many other young people in various parts of the world, you will be told that changes must be made, that you must have more freedom, that you should be different from your parents, and that the decisions about your lives depend on you, and you alone.

The prospect of growing economic progress, and the chance of obtaining a greater share of the goods that modern society has to offer, will appear to you as an opportunity to achieve greater freedom. The more you possess – you may be tempted to think – the more you will feel liberated from every type of confinement. In order to make more money and to possess more, in order to eliminate effort and worry, you may be tempted to take moral shortcuts where honesty, truth and work are concerned. The progress of science and technology seems inevitable and you may be enticed to look towards the technological society for the answers to all your problems.

The lure of pleasure, to be had whenever and wherever it can be found, will be strong and it may be presented to you as part of progress towards greater autonomy and freedom from rules. The desire to be free from external restraints may manifest itself very strongly in the sexual domain, since this is an area that is so closely tied to a human personality. The moral standards that the Church and society have held up to you for so long a time, will be presented as obsolete and a hindrance to the full development of your own personality. Mass media, entertainment, and literature will present a model for living where all too often it is every man for himself, and where the unrestrained affirmation of self leaves no room for concern for others.

You will hear people tell you that your religious practices are hopelessly out of date, that they hamper your style and your future, that with everything that social and scientific progress has to offer, you will be able to organise your own lives, and that God has played out his role. Even many religious persons will adopt such attitudes, breathing them in from the surrounding atmosphere, without attending to the practical atheism that is at their origin.

A society that, in this way, has lost its higher religious and moral principles will become an easy prey for manipulation and for domination by the forces which, under the pretext of greater freedom, will enslave it ever more. How many young people have already warped their consciences and have substituted the true joy of life with drugs, sex, alcohol, vandalism and the empty pursuit of mere material possessions?

Something else is needed: something that you will find only in Christ, for he alone is the measure and the scale that you must use to evaluate your own life. Christ keeps calling you, he keeps inviting you, but he calls you in truth. His call is demanding, for he taught us what it means to be truly human. Without heeding the call of Jesus, it will not be possible to realise the fullness of your own humanity. You must build on the foundation which is Christ; only with him your life will be meaningful and worthwhile.

Permit me to recall still another phrase of the Gospel that Christ pronounced in the Sermon on the Mount: 'Love your enemies, do good to those who hate you' (Lk 6: 27). I have before my mind the painful events that for over 10 years have been taking place in Northern Ireland. These events, painful as they are, must also be an incitement to reflection. They demand that you form an interior judgement of conscience to determine where you, as young Catholics, stand on the matter.

The command of Jesus does not mean that we are not bound by love for our native land; it does not mean that we can remain indifferent before injustice in its various temporal and historical aspects. These words of Jesus take away only hate. I beg you to reflect deeply: what would the world be if in our mutual relations we were to give primacy to hatred among people, between classes, between nations? What would the future of humanity be if we were to base on this hatred the future of individuals and of nations?

Sometimes, one could have the feeling that, before the experiences of history and before concrete situations, love has lost its power and that it is impossible to practise it. And yet, in the long run, love always brings victory, love is never defeated. And, I could add, the history of Ireland proves that, if it were not so, humanity would only be condemned to destruction.

Dear young friends … tell your parents, and everyone who wants to listen, that the Pope believes in you and that he counts on you. Say that the young are the strength of the Pope, who wishes to share with them his hope for the future and his encouragement.

I have given you the words of my heart. The future of all peoples and nations, the future of humanity itself depends on this: whether the words of Jesus in the Sermon on the Mount, whether the message of the Gospel will be listened to once again.

May the Lord Jesus be always with you! With his truth that makes you free; with his word that unlocks the mystery of man and reveals to man his own humanity; with his death and Resurrection that makes you new and strong.

Young people of Ireland, I love you! Young people of Ireland, I bless you! I bless you in the name of our Lord Jesus Christ.

Críost liom, Críost romham, Críost i mo dhiaidh.

Charles J. Haughey
(1925–2006)

A native of Castlebar, County Mayo, Charles Haughey was one of Ireland's most colourful politicians in the final quarter of the 20th century. He became leader of Fianna Fáil in 1977 and served four terms as Taoiseach between 1979 and 1992, when he resigned. Despite public disquiet about his own finances (he lived well beyond his visible means), he is credited with securing Ireland's economy in the 1990s by imposing stringent cutbacks in public services and implementing other belt-tightening measures. During 1979 Ireland had been plagued by industrial action, much of it in the services sector.

'What we need is a new way forward.'

Charles Haughey at the microphone.

From a broadcast on RTÉ television, 9 January 1980

I wish to talk to you this evening about the state of the nation's affairs and the picture I have to paint is not, unfortunately, a very cheerful one.

The figures which are just now becoming available to us show one thing very clearly. As a community we are living away beyond our means. I do not mean that everyone in the community is living too well. Clearly many are not and have barely enough to get by. But taking us all together, we have been living at a rate which is simply not justified by the amount of goods and services we are producing.

To make up the difference, we have been borrowing enormous amounts of money, borrowing at a rate which just cannot continue. A few simple figures will make this very clear.

At home, the government's current income from taxes and all other sources in 1979 fell short of what was needed to pay the running costs of the state by about £520 million. To meet this and our capital programme, we had to borrow in 1979 over £100 million. That amount is equal to one-seventh of our entire national output for the year. This is just far too high a rate and cannot possibly continue.

The situation in regard to our trading with the outside world in 1979 was bad also. Our income from abroad fell short of what we had to pay out by about £760 million which led to a fall in our reserves.

To fully understand the situation, we must look not just on the home scene but also on the troubled and unstable world around us. There are wars and rumours of wars. There is political instability in some of the most important areas of the world. A very serious threat exists to the world's future supply of energy. We can no longer be sure that we will be able to go on paying the prices now being demanded for all the oil and other fuels we require to keep our factories going and to keep our homes and institutions supplied with the light, heat and power they need. We will, of course, push exploration for our own oil ahead as rapidly as possible but in the short term the burden of oil prices will continue to be a crushing one.

All this indicates that we must, first of all, as a matter of urgency, set about putting our domestic affairs in order and secondly, improving our trade with the rest of the world in so far as we can do so.

We will have to continue to cut down on government spending. The government is taking far too much by way of taxes from individual members of the community. But even this amount is not enough to meet our commitments. We will just have to reorganise government spending so that we can only undertake the things which we can afford.

In trying to bring government expenditure within manageable proportions, we will, of course, be paying particular attention to the needs of the poorer and weaker sections of the community and make sure they are looked after. Other essential community expenditure will have to be undertaken also. But there are many things which will just have to be curtailed or postponed, until such time as we can get the financial situation right.

There is one thing above all else which we can do to help get the situation right and which is entirely within our control. I refer to industrial relations. Any further serious interruption in production, or in the provision of essential services, in 1980 would be a major disaster. I believe that everyone listening to me tonight shares my anxiety about our situation in this respect.

Strikes, go-slows, work-to-rule, stoppages in key industries and essential services were too often a feature of life in 1979. They caused suffering and hardship; at times it looked as if we were becoming one of those countries where basic services could not be relied on to operate as part of normal life.

Immediately following my election as taoiseach, I received countless messages from all over the country from people in every walk of life, appealing to me to do something about this situation.

Let us clearly understand, however, that this is not a one-sided affair. Managements that do not give first-class attention to their firm's industrial relations, who ignore situations and let them drift into confrontation, are just as blameworthy as the handful of wild men who slap on an unofficial picket and stop thousands of workers from earning their living.

Apportioning blame, however, is not going to let us get anywhere. What we need is a new way forward and that is my primary purpose, as head of government, in talking to you tonight.

I am asking for a universal commitment to industrial peace in 1980. I am asking every worker and employer, every trade union, every employers' organisation, every farmer and every farming organisation, every housewife, in fact every industrial citizen, to play a part in ending this humiliating, destructive industrial strife and putting in its place discussion, negotiations and peaceful settlements.

Joe Connolly
(b. 1956)

Joe Connolly began his hurling career at
school in St Mary's College, Galway. A
Hurler of the Year and a GAA All-Star, he
captained the Galway team to victory in the
1980 Senior Hurling All-Ireland final. Mirroring
Pope John Paul's famous declaration to the
young people of Ireland in 1979, Connolly paid tribute in his
acceptance speech – delivered in Irish – to the people of Galway
and all those Galwegians who had emigrated to Britain and the
US over the years.

'People of Galway – we love you!'

Joe Connolly lifts the cup in the 1980 Senior Hurling All-Ireland final.

Speech accepting the Liam McCarthy Cup at Croke Park, Dublin, 7 September 1980

*A*mhunitir na Gaillimhe, tar éis seacht mbliana agus caoga tá Craobh na hÉireann ar ais i nGaillimh. Is mór an onóir domsa mar chaptaen an corn seo a ghlacadh ar son an fhoireann uilig.

Is iontach an lá inniu le bheith mar Ghaillmheach. Tá daoine ar ais in nGaillimh agus tá gliondar ina gcroí. Ach freisin caithfimid cuimhneamh ar d[h]aoine I Sasana, I Meiriceá, ar fuaid na tire. Agus tá siad, b' fhéidir, ag caoineadh anois i láthair.

(Ba mhaith liom freisin buíochas) a ghabháil do fhoireann Luimnigh as ucht an cluiche iontach a thug siad dúinn inniu. People of Galway – we love you!

[People of Galway, after 57 years the all-Ireland [trophy] is back in Galway. It is a great honour for me as captain to accept this cup on behalf of all the team.

It is a wonderful day to be from Galway. There are people back in Galway and there is joy in their hearts. But we also have to remember people in England, in America, throughout the country. And they are, perhaps, crying [with joy] at the moment.

(I would also like to thank) the Limerick team for the wonderful game they gave us today.]

Galway selector Joe Connolly.

John Hume
(b. 1937)

John Hume, a native of Derry, was a founding member of the Social Democratic and Labour Party (SDLP) in 1970. He became its leader in 1979, and was elected MP in 1983. Committed to conciliation between unionists and nationalists, he began a dialogue with Gerry Adams in 1988 that eventually paved the way to the peace process in Northern Ireland. In 1998 he was awarded the Nobel Peace Prize, jointly with David Trimble, after the signing of the Belfast Agreement. When Margaret Thatcher and Garret FitzGerald agreed to a programme of rolling devolution for Northern Ireland in 1981, nationalist and unionist extremists seemed intent on pulling Ulster into a cataclysm of violence. Hume's speech to the SDLP's annual party conference was an appeal to moderates on both sides.

'Sit down and negotiate our future with us.'

From a speech at the SDLP annual party conference, Newcastle, County Down, 14 November 1981

I would say this to the Protestants of Northern Ireland: many among you can have little satisfaction in seeing the steady rise in tyrannical dominance over you of a man whose name in every country in the world has become a byword for bigotry, demagoguery and obscurantism. Is Paisleyism in any sense consistent with those great Protestant values of individual freedom and free speech of which you are so rightly proud? Is not what is being said and done in your name in Northern Ireland a gross and unworthy abuse of everything you stand for?

The essence of the appeal of unionism is that it is the only protection of Protestants in Ireland. Is it? Has it not instead seriously weakened your integrity and become a profound source politically and intellectually of real danger to the deepest values of the Protestant tradition in Ireland? Is it not time to consider that there are other ways, not only to protect the integrity of your tradition but to develop it and become a positive leaven in Irish society, challenging its uniformity? Is it not time to recognise that there are other ways that do not involve conflict with your neighbours on this island but a fruitful partnership which recognises the richness of difference and diversity? Surely not to consider other ways is to consign your own future, your children's future, our future, to despair, and surely you have no more right than we do to adopt such a nihilistic course. Must you – and now absurdly – permit your leaders to demand all power, exclusively and forever? For ourselves, we abjure any 'solution' in which there would be winners and losers, conquerors and vanquished, victory and defeat. So should you. Face reality with us and let us together be grateful that we have an opportunity to do so before catastrophe – which loomed over us earlier this year – overwhelms us all.

All we demand is that you and your leaders sit down and negotiate our future with us and the British and Irish governments. For our part, we would insist that the results of such talks would have to be ratified in two separate referenda, one in the North, the other in the South. The principle of consent will be truly respected. We have to live together in the future. I know that many of you do not fully grasp my words. I know that you do not realise that when we say we are proposing an 'Agreed Ireland' we mean those words absolutely literally. We mean an 'Agreed Ireland' which you would decisively help to shape.

The nationalists of the North see in the Provisionals' activity the destruction of the integrity of their own political values, a direct attack on the real meaning of Irish unity. We also see in those parts of the community where the Provisional IRA are most active, the spread of a foul social cancer. The coherence of society at the best of times is both deep-rooted and fragile. The roots, the shared principles of respect for life, liberty and order, can go deep but they must be tended and watered assiduously and incessantly. There are now communities in Northern Ireland where these roots have not alone been neglected, but have been hacked away and poisoned by the Provisional IRA's campaign against fundamental human rights to live until God calls us. What has followed is a gross distortion of moral values in society, the promotion of the pornography of death and nihilism on our gable walls and the deep corruption of the young. The SDLP will always recognise this evil for what it is and call it by its name: murder.

We say to the Provisionals, you are not Irish republicans, you are extremists who have dishonoured and are dishonouring the deepest ideals of the Irish people. Can we remind you yet again that those whose inheritance you so falsely claim, laid down their arms in 1916 lest they cause any undue suffering to their Irish people.

We as a party remain committed to a noble art – politics. Politics has been described as many things. Its essence is the reconciliation of differences – the greatest challenge facing the people of the community today. 'No man is good enough to govern another,' said Lincoln 'without that other man's consent.' The challenge of building a consensus in Ireland is the greatest challenge in particular to this new generation, a challenge that is all the more exciting because of the failure of previous generations to meet it. It is a challenge that will only be met by patient political negotiation. Patient political negotiation is unspectacular, it has no dramatic appeal.

The alternative – the use of violence disguised as military patriotism – has misled many young idealists. Its monuments are mangled and broken bodies, prison walls and cemeteries. Patient political effort will not fill graves – violence will. Patient political effort will not fill jails with young people. Violence will. Patient political effort will not prevent job creation in a community starved of employment, particularly for young people. Violence will. Patient political effort and non-violence have only achievements and benefits that we can claim over the past decade. Violence has made the underlying problem – division – more difficult to solve.

Many young people have joined us in the task of politics, the difficult task of building mutual respect and understanding which forms the basis of true peace and freedom. We need many more. In the 1980s the true patriot is the builder, not the destroyer. 1981 has been a year of many lessons for many people. The SDLP has come through 1981. We hope that we shall never see its like again. Yet we have emerged with renewed strength. We can only go forward.

Secretary Clinton with
Nobel Peace Prize
Winners David Trimble
and John Hume

Des O'Malley
(b. 1939)

The Limerick-born Fianna Fáil TD was a vigorous opponent of Charles Haughey during the Arms Crisis of 1970 and in the attempts to oust Haughey from government. In the 1980s the Catholic Church in Ireland held sway over the private morals of Irish citizens and the sale of contraceptives was still banned. In 1985 the minister for health introduced legislation allowing the sale of non-medical contraceptives and Haughey refused to allow Fianna Fáil TDs a free vote. O'Malley was the only one of their number who refused to vote with the party against the bill. He was expelled from Fianna Fáil for conduct unbecoming in that debate, and he established his own party, the Progressive Democrats. The party later formed a coalition with Fianna Fáil, under Haughey, in 1989. In 1992 O'Malley was instrumental in toppling Haughey, who resigned as taoiseach.

'Allow citizens to make their own free choice.'

Des O'Malley in pensive mood at an interview.

From his speech to Dáil Éireann on the Family Planning Bill, 20 February 1985

There are certain fundamental matters which far transcend the details of this bill and which are of grave importance to democracy on this island.

In many respects this debate can be regarded as a sort of watershed in Irish politics. It will have a considerable influence on the whole political institutional, democratic future, not just of these 26 counties but of the whole island. We must approach the subject very seriously and bearing that in mind. It is right to ask ourselves now what would be the reaction and the effect of this bill being defeated this evening. I am not interested in the reaction or the effect so far as contraception is concerned because that is no longer relevant. If the bill is defeated there are two elements on this island who will rejoice to high heaven. They are the unionists in Northern Ireland and the extremist Roman Catholics in the Republic. They are a curious alliance, but they are bound together by the vested interest each of them has in the perpetuation of partition. Neither wishes to know the other. Their wish is to keep this island divided. Most of us here realise that the imposition of partition on this island was a grievous wrong, but its deliberate continuation is equally a grievous wrong. No one who wishes that this island, this race and this nation be united again should try to have this division copper fastened. It does not matter what any of us might like to say to ourselves about what might be the effects of the availability of condoms or anything else, what really matters and what will matter in 10, 20 or 30 years' time is whether the elected representatives of the Irish people decided they wished to underwrite, at least mentally, the concept of partition.

Most of us in the House fervently want to see a 32-county republic on this island. I am not as optimistic as I used to be about that – I think the day is further away than it might otherwise be because of the events of the last 10 or 15 years. I am certain of one thing in relation to partition: we will never see a 32-county republic on this island until first of all we have here a 26-county republic in the part we have jurisdiction over today which is really a republic, practising real republican traditions. Otherwise, we can forget about the possibility of ever succeeding in persuading our fellow Irishmen in the North to join us.

In a democratic republic people should not think in terms of having laws other than those that allow citizens to make their own free choice in so far as these private matters are concerned. That is what I believe a republic should do. It should take account of the reasonable views of all groups, including all minorities, because if we do not take into account the rights of minorities here, can we complain if they are not taken into account in the other part of the island, or anywhere else.

This whole matter affects me personally and politically. I have thought about it and agonised about it. Quite a number of deputies have been subjected to a particular type of pressure, but I am possibly unique in that I have been subjected to two enormous pressures, the more general type and a particular political one. But it comes down to certain fundamentals. One has to take into account everything that has been said but one must also act in accordance with one's conscience, not on contraceptives, which is irrelevant now, but on the bigger and deeper issues.

I will conclude by quoting from a letter in *The Irish Times* of 16 February, signed by Father Dominic Johnson OSB, a monk of Glenstal Abbey, where he says, 'With respect to Mr O'Malley, he might reflect with profit on the life of St Thomas More, who put his conscience before politics and lost his life for doing so.'

The politics of this would be very easy. The politics would be to be one of the lads, the safest way in Ireland. But I do not believe that the interests of this state, or our constitution and of this Republic, would be served by putting politics before conscience in regard to this. There is a choice of a kind that can only be answered by saying that I stand by the Republic and accordingly I will not oppose this bill.

Garret FitzGerald
(1926–2011)

Son of the Irish Free State's first foreign minister, Garret FitzGerald was elected to Dáil Éireann in 1969 and was appointed minister for foreign affairs in 1973. Taoiseach for two terms in the 1980s, he resigned as Fine Gael party leader in 1987 and retired from politics in 1992. His greatest legacy was the Anglo-Irish Agreement of 1985, which provided a foundation for the 1998 Good Friday Agreement and the present power-sharing administration in Northern Ireland. In the 1980s the constitutional ban on divorce, so vehemently opposed by W. B. Yeats in 1925, was still in place. FitzGerald announced a 'constitutional crusade' against anything that Protestants in the North found unacceptable in the constitution of the Irish Republic.

'Our people are entitled to a mature discussion.'

Dr Garrett Fitzgerald in 1989.

From his speech to Dáil Éireann on the repeal of the constitutional ban on divorce, 16 May 1986

A s legislators elected by the people, we have a duty of leadership in relation to this matter as we have in other matters; and we in the parties in government are exercising this leadership by proposing a very restrictive form of divorce with a minimal impact on existing marriages, which will at the same time reduce the destabilising effect of marriage breakdown on society, so as to increase the stability of family life in our society.

On the merits of this proposition there are not merely deeply divided opinions; there are deeply divided approaches to the whole matter, involving the application of quite different criteria to the issue involved. The first of these involves the application of the criterion of the social good. I believe that this is the most important criterion that we should apply, because of the social nature of marriage itself.

A second approach emphasises the importance of respect for diversity of opinion and for freedom under the law. These are very important values which must command the respect of the state, in conjunction with the issue of the social good.

A third approach emphasises the importance of compassion in human affairs. Despite the old adage that bad cases make bad law, we cannot ignore this human value, which must be given its place within the overall social good.

A fourth approach, which has the support of a minority here even though it has been repeatedly repudiated by the authorities of the Roman Catholic Church, is that the theology and law of that church should be the foundation of, or even constitute the content of, the civil law of our state. While personally committed to the indissoluble character of sacramental marriage in the church of which I am a member, I reject that approach, in common with the authorities of my church and the vast majority of the Irish people.

In this debate we should try to disentangle these different approaches and to consider what weight should be given to each of them. Otherwise the debate could be a dialogue of the deaf, involving nothing more than repetitive reassertions of extreme positions. On the one side there could be a series of reiterations of the 'conservative' position, namely, that divorce is contrary to the theology, and at variance with the ecclesiastical law of the Roman Catholic Church, and that it would destabilise society – without any consideration of the alternative social danger that our society might be even more destabilised by a continuation of the present situation.

On the other side there could be an equally tedious reiteration of the 'liberal' position that there is an individual 'right' to divorce – without regard either to the losses as well as gains involved for individuals, or to the possible social consequences of a change in the status quo.

I recognise that no single contribution to the discussion, nor even a sustained effort to secure rational debate, will necessarily succeed in an area that arouses such strong emotions on either side. But it is our duty in this House as elected leaders of opinion, responsible for the common good and for the protection of individual rights, to attempt to place the debate on a rational level, and to follow, indeed, the good advice of the Roman Catholic hierarchy that 'in this debate opposing views should be fairly stated and honestly listened to and appraised'.

Our people are entitled to such a mature discussion in their Parliament. They are entitled to the considered advice of their legislators as to the impact of this constitutional amendment on marriage and on our society.

In conclusion, I believe that this debate has also an importance that extends outside the boundaries of this state. The type of provision we are proposing to make for divorce takes account of lessons to be learned from other countries, and may, I believe, come to be seen elsewhere as a balanced and mature approach to a difficult problem. This debate, and the subsequent wider public discussion, together with the eventual decision taken by the people of this state, will, of course, be watched particularly closely by people of both traditions in Northern Ireland, many of whom will, I believe, be influenced to a degree in their attitude towards this state and towards each other by the manner in which we act in this matter.

That will not be a primary consideration when this matter is put to the test. But it should not be ignored either. And to the extent that electors conclude that this proposal should be adopted on its own merits to meet the social needs of this state, to that extent they will also be helping incidentally the relationship between North and South and between the communities in Northern Ireland. At a time when the situation in Northern Ireland is so delicately balanced this is not something we can reasonably ignore.

Mary Robinson
(b. 1944)

Ireland's first female president was born in County Mayo and trained as a lawyer. A member of the Seanad for 20 years, she was elected to the presidency as the Labour candidate in 1990, the first time that Labour had contested a presidential election. She resigned in 1997 and was appointed United Nations High Commissioner on Human Rights, a position she held until 2002. Throughout her career she has been a supporter of and campaigner for a wide range of liberal issues.

'The West's awake.'

Mary Robinson at the World Economic Forum.

From her inaugural address as President of Ireland, Dublin Castle, 3 December 1990

itizens of Ireland, *mná na hÉireann agus fir na hÉireann,* you have chosen me to represent you and I am humbled by and grateful for your trust. The Ireland I will be representing is a new Ireland, open, tolerant, inclusive. Many of you who voted for me did so without sharing all my views. This, I believe, is a significant signal of change, a sign, however modest, that we have already passed the threshold to a new, pluralist Ireland.

The recent revival of an old concept of the Fifth Province expresses this emerging Ireland of tolerance and empathy. The old Irish term for province is coicead, meaning 'fifth'; and yet, as everyone knows, there are only four geographical provinces on this island. So where is the fifth? The Fifth Province is not anywhere here or there, north or south, east or west. It is a place within each of us – that place that is open to the other, that swinging door which allows us to venture out and others to venture in. Ancient legends divide Ireland into four quarters and a 'middle', although they differed about the location of this middle or Fifth Province. While Tara was the political centre of Ireland, tradition has it that this Fifth Province acted as a second centre, a necessary balance. If I am a symbol of anything I would like to be a symbol of this reconciling and healing Fifth Province.

My primary role as president will be to represent this state. But this state is not the only model of community with which Irish people can and do identify. Beyond our state there is a vast community of Irish emigrants extending not only across our neighbouring island – which has provided a home away from home for several Irish generations – but also throughout the continents of North America, Australia and of course Europe itself. There are over 70 million people living on this globe who claim Irish descent. I will be proud to represent them. And I would like to see Áras an Uachtaráin, my official residence, serve – on something of an annual basis – as a place where our emigrant communities could send representatives for a get-together of the extended Irish family abroad.

If it is time, as Joyce's Stephen Dedalus remarked, that the Irish began to forge in the smithy of our souls 'the uncreated conscience of our race' – might we not take on the still 'uncreated conscience' of the wider international community? Is it not time that the small started believing again that it is beautiful, that the periphery can rise up and speak out on equal terms with the centre, that the most outlying island community of the European Community really has something 'strange and precious' to contribute to the sea-change presently sweeping through the entire continent of Europe? As a native of Ballina, one of the most western towns of the most western province of the most western nation in Europe, I want to say – 'the West's awake'.

I turn now to another place close to my heart, Northern Ireland. As the elected choice of the people of this part of our island I want to extend the hand of friendship and of love to both communities in the other part. And I want to do this with no hidden agendas, no strings attached. As the person chosen by you to symbolise this Republic and to project our self-image to others, I will seek to encourage mutual understanding and tolerance between all the different communities sharing this island.

In seeking to do this I shall rely to a large extent on symbols. But symbols are what unite and divide people. Symbols give us our identity, our self-image, our way of explaining ourselves to ourselves and to others. Symbols in turn determine the kinds of stories we tell; and the stories we tell determine the kind of history we make and remake. I want Áras an Uachtaráin to be a place where people can tell diverse stories – in the knowledge that there is someone there to listen.

I want this presidency to promote the telling of stories – stories of celebration through the arts and stories of conscience and of social justice. As a woman, I want women who have felt themselves outside history to be written back into history, in the words of Eavan Boland, 'finding a voice where they found a vision'.

May God direct me so that my presidency is one of justice, peace and love. May I have the fortune to preside over an Ireland at a time of exciting transformation when we enter a new Europe where old wounds can be healed, a time when, in the words of Seamus Heaney, 'hope and history rhyme'. May it be a presidency where I, the president, can sing to you, citizens of Ireland, the joyous refrain of the 14th-century Irish poet as recalled by W. B. Yeats, 'I am of Ireland … come dance with me in Ireland.'

Mary Robinson with healthworker Nadhifa Ibrahim Mohamed in Somalia.

Máire Geoghegan-Quinn
(b. 1950)

The daughter of a Fianna Fáil TD for Galway West, Máire Geoghegan-Quinn was the first woman in the history of the state to hold a cabinet position when she was appointed minister for the Gaeltacht in 1979. In 1991, in protest against Charles Haughey's leadership, she resigned from government. In 1988 the European Court of Human Rights had delivered a judgment that required the government to decriminalise homosexual acts between consenting adults, but it wasn't until 1993, when Geoghegan-Quinn became minister for justice, that legislation conforming with the judgment was proposed.

'We have come to appreciate the need to recognise, respect and value difference.'

Máire Geoghegan-Quinn delivers a speech at an EU event.

From her speech to Dáil Éireann supporting the bill to decriminalise sexual acts between consenting male adults, 23 June 1993

W hat we are concerned with fundamentally in this bill is a necessary development of human rights. We are seeking to end that form of discrimination which says that those whose nature is to express themselves sexually in their personal relationships, as consenting adults, in a way which others disapprove of or feel uneasy about, must suffer the sanctions of the criminal law. We are saying in 1993, over 130 years since this section of the criminal law was enacted, that it is time we brought this form of human rights limitation to an end. We are recognising that we are in an era in which values are being examined and questioned and that it is no more than our duty as legislators to show that we appreciate what is happening by dismantling a law which reflects the values of another time.

That process of change is not easy and, understandably, many people worry that the traditional values which they hold so dear, and many of which are fundamentally sound, are under siege from emerging modern realities. But, of course, it is not a matter of laying siege to all the old certainties, nor is it a matter of jettisoning sound values simply to run with the current tide of demand, which may or may not be a majority demand. It is, rather, a matter of looking closely at values and asking ourselves whether it is necessary, or right, that they be propped up for the comfort of the majority by applying discriminatory and unnecessary laws to a minority, any minority.

As a people we have proved our ability to adopt a balanced and mature approach in dealing with complex social issues. In this context I am particularly pleased to note that, by and large, the public debate which has taken place in relation to the area covered by the bill has been marked by a lack of stridency and by a respect for the sincerity of the views held by others.

Because some of the issues raised by this bill are ones on which many people have deeply and sincerely held opposing views, it is perhaps inevitable that in the public debate the reality of what the bill actually proposes to do can sometimes be lost sight of in the context of wider issues which tend to be raised. For this reason it is important to emphasise that the House is not being asked to take a view as to whether sexual behaviour of the kind dealt with in the main sections of the bill should be regarded as morally or socially acceptable. Instead, what is simply at issue is whether it is right in this day and age that the full force and sanctions of the criminal law should be available in relation to such forms of sexual behaviour.

Majority values do not require that kind of support and I believe this is something that each of us knows instinctively. We know in ourselves also that values which are truly worthwhile in themselves are strengthened – not weakened – when we remove forms of apparent support which ignore the rights of others. In other areas of public concern and debate in this country we have come to appreciate the need to recognise, respect and value difference. This House needs no reminding of the tragedy which ensues when difference is deprived of the right of expression and suppressed.

I do not believe that it is any answer to say that in practice these laws are rarely if ever implemented and we would be best to leave well enough alone. Such an approach would be dishonest, could bring the law generally into disrepute and, it seems to me, would be grossly and gratuitously offensive to those who happen to be homosexual. Genuine tolerance is not achieved by the turning of a blind eye. The social acceptability of homosexuality is not something which by our laws we can decree; the hurt which homosexuals feel at their treatment as outcasts by some members of the community is not something which we can dispel by the use of some legislative magic wand. What we can do under the terms of this bill is leave those of homosexual orientation free to come to terms with their lives and express themselves in personal relationships without fear of being branded and being punished as criminals.

Seamus Heaney
(1939–2013)

The son of a small farmer in County Derry, Seamas Heaney was a poet, academic and Nobel laureate. His earlier work dealt with the Northern 'troubles' from a Catholic perspective and he had been in the running for the Nobel award for many years before he received it in 1995. Although his work had moved on to other topics, the Nobel committee singled out his 'Northern' work for special commendation.

'The Ireland I now inhabit.'

From his Nobel acceptance speech in Stockholm, 7 December 1995

When the poet W. B. Yeats stood on this platform more than 70 years ago, Ireland was emerging from the throes of a traumatic civil war that had followed fast on the heels of a war of independence fought against the British. The struggle that ensued had been brief enough; it was over by May, 1923, some seven months before Yeats sailed to Stockholm, but it was bloody, savage and intimate, and for generations to come it would dictate the terms of politics within the 26 independent counties of Ireland, that part of the island known first of all as the Irish Free State and then subsequently as the Republic of Ireland.

Yeats barely alluded to the civil war or the war of independence in his Nobel speech. Nobody understood better than he the connection between the construction or destruction of state institutions and the founding or foundering of cultural life, but on this occasion he chose to talk instead about the Irish Dramatic Movement. His story was about the creative purpose of that movement and its historic good fortune in having not only his own genius to sponsor it, but also the genius of his friends John Millington Synge and Lady Augusta Gregory. He came to Sweden to tell the world that the local work of poets and dramatists had been as important to the transformation of his native place and times as the ambushes of guerrilla armies; and his boast in that elevated prose was essentially the same as the one he would make in verse more than a decade later in his poem 'The municipal gallery revisited'. There Yeats presents himself amongst the portraits and heroic narrative paintings which celebrate the events and personalities of recent history and all of a sudden realises that something truly epoch-making has occurred: '"This is not", I say,/"the dead Ireland of my youth, but an Ireland/The poets have imagined, terrible and gay."' And the poem concludes with two of the most quoted lines of his entire oeuvre:

Think where man's glory most begins and ends,

And say my glory was I had such friends.

And yet, expansive and thrilling as these lines are, they are an instance of poetry flourishing itself rather than proving itself, they are the poet's lap of honour, and in this respect if in no other they resemble what I am doing in this lecture. In fact, I should quote here on my own behalf other words from the poem: 'You that would judge me, do not judge alone/This book or that.' Instead I ask you to do what Yeats asked his audience to do and think of the achievement of

Irish poets and dramatists and novelists over the past 40 years, among whom I am proud to count great friends.

In literary matters, Ezra Pound advised against accepting the opinion of those 'who haven't themselves produced notable work', and it is advice I have been privileged to follow, since it is the good opinion of notable workers and not just those in my own country that has fortified my endeavour since I began to write in Belfast more than 30 years ago. The Ireland I now inhabit is one that these Irish contemporaries have helped to imagine.

Seamus Heaney speaking at the launch of Library Ireland Week 2010

David Trimble

(b. 1944)

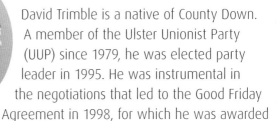

David Trimble is a native of County Down. A member of the Ulster Unionist Party (UUP) since 1979, he was elected party leader in 1995. He was instrumental in the negotiations that led to the Good Friday Agreement in 1998, for which he was awarded the Nobel Prize for Peace, jointly with John Hume. He was Northern Ireland's first minister twice, but resigned as the leader of the UUP when it was defeated in the 2005 election by the Democratic Unionist Party.

'Winter is here, and there is still no sign of spring.'

From his Nobel acceptance speech, Oslo, 10 December 1998

Common sense dictates that I cannot for ever convince society that real peace is at hand if there is not a beginning to the decommissioning of weapons as an earnest of the decommissioning of hearts that must follow. Any further delay will reinforce dark doubts about whether Sinn Féin are drinking from the clear stream of democracy, or are still drinking from the dark stream of fascism. It cannot for ever face both ways. Plenty of space has been given to the paramilitaries. Now, winter is here, and there is still no sign of spring.

What we democratic politicians want in Northern Ireland is not some utopian society but a normal society. The best way to secure that normalcy is the tried and trusted method of parliamentary democracy. So the Northern Ireland Assembly is the primary institutional instrument for the development of a normal society in Northern Ireland. Like any Parliament it needs to be more than a cockpit for competing victimisations. Burke said it best, 'Parliament is not a congress of ambassadors from different and hostile interests; which interests each must maintain, as an agent and an advocate, against other agents and advocates; but Parliament is a deliberative assembly of one nation, with one interest, that of the whole; where not local purposes, nor local prejudices ought to guide, but the general good resulting from the general reason of the whole.'

Some critics complain that I lack 'the vision thing'. But vision in its pure meaning is clear sight. That does not mean I have no dreams. I do. But I try to have them at night. By day I am satisfied if I can see the furthest limit of what is possible. Politics can be likened to driving at night over unfamiliar hills and mountains. There are hills in Northern Ireland and there are mountains. The hills are decommissioning and policing. But the mountain, if we could but see it clearly, is not in front of us, but behind us, in history. The dark shadow we seem to see in the distance is not really a mountain ahead, but the shadow of the mountain behind – a shadow from the past thrown forward into our future. It is a dark sludge of historical sectarianism. We can leave it behind if we wish.

But both communities must leave it behind, because both created it. Each thought it had good reason to fear the other. As Namier says, the irrational is not necessarily unreasonable. Ulster Unionists, fearful of being isolated on the island, built a solid house, but it was a cold house for Catholics. And northern nationalists, although they had a roof over their heads, seemed to us as if they meant to burn the house down. None of us are entirely innocent. But thanks to our strong sense of civil society, thanks to our religious recognition that none of us are perfect, thanks to the thousands of people from both sides who made countless acts of good authority, thanks to a tradition of parliamentary democracy which meant that paramilitarism never displaced politics, thanks to all these specific, concrete circumstances we, thank God, stopped short of that abyss that engulfed Bosnia, Kosovo, Somalia and Rwanda. There are two traditions in Northern Ireland. There are two main religious denominations. But there is only one true moral denomination. And it wants peace.

Tony Blair
(b. 1953)

In 1997 Tony Blair, the leader of the British
Labour Party, became the youngest British
prime minister in almost 200 years when
Labour won a landslide victory in the
general election. On 26 November 1998
he became the first British prime minister to
address the Irish parliament, created 80 years earlier in defiance
of the British government. In his historic speech, Blair spoke
of his own Irish roots, and of the ground-breaking Good Friday
Agreement as signalling an end to over 800 years of enmity
between Britain and Ireland.

'The shared hope of a new beginning.'

From his speech to the joint Houses of the Oireachtas, 26 December 1998

After all the long and torn history of our two peoples, standing here as the first British prime minister ever to address the joint Houses of the Oireachtas, I feel profoundly both the history in this event, and I feel profoundly the enormity of the honour that you are bestowing upon me. From the bottom of my heart, *go raibh míle maith agaibh.*

Like it or not, we, the British and the Irish, are irredeemably linked. Celts, Vikings, Normans – all left their distinctive mark on our countries. Over a thousand years ago, the monastic traditions formed the basis for both our cultures. Sadly, the power games of medieval monarchs and feudal chiefs sowed the seeds of later trouble.

Yet it has always been simplistic to portray our differences as simply Irish versus English – or British. There were, after all, many in Britain too who suffered greatly at the hands of powerful absentee landlords, who were persecuted for their religion, or who were for centuries disenfranchised. And each generation in Britain has benefited, as ours does, from the contribution of Irish men and women.

So much shared history, so much shared pain. And now the shared hope of a new beginning.

The peace process is at a difficult juncture. Progress is being made, but slowly. There is an impasse over the establishment of the executive; there is an impasse over decommissioning. But I have been optimistic the whole way through. And I am optimistic now. Let us not underestimate how far we have come; and let us agree that we have come too far to go back now.

Politics is replacing violence as the way people do business. The Good Friday Agreement holds out the prospect of a peaceful long-term future for Northern Ireland, and the whole island of Ireland. The Northern Ireland Bill provides for the new Assembly and Executive, the North-South Ministerial Council, and the British-Irish Council. It incorporates the principle of consent into British constitutional law and repeals the Government of Ireland Act of 1920. It establishes a Human Rights Commission with the power to support individual cases. We will have an Equality Commission to police a new duty on all public bodies in Northern Ireland to promote equality of opportunity. We have set up the Patten Commission to review policing. We are scaling down the military presence. Prisoners are being released.

None of this is easy. I get many letters from the victims of violence asking why we are freeing terrorist prisoners. It is a tough question but my answer is clear: the agreement would never have come about if we had not tackled the issue of prisoners. That agreement heralds the prospect of an end to violence and a peaceful future for Northern Ireland. Our duty is to carry it out. That is a duty I feel more strongly than ever, having seen for myself the horror of Omagh. This was not the first such atrocity. But with all of my being, I will it to be the last.

In Belfast or Dublin, people say the same thing: make the agreement work.

Don't believe anyone who says the British people don't care about the peace process. People in my country care deeply about it, are willing it to work. And in our two countries, it is not just the politicians who have a role to play.

No one should ignore the injustices of the past, or the lessons of history. But too often between us, one person's history has been another person's myth.

We need not be prisoners of our history. My generation in Britain sees Ireland differently today and probably the same generation here feels differently about Britain.

Different traditions have to understand each other. Just as we must understand your yearning for a united Ireland, so too must you understand what the best of unionism is about. They are good and decent people, just like you. They want to remain part of the UK – and I have made it clear that I value that wish. They feel threatened. Threatened by the terrorism with which they have had to live for so long. Threatened, until the Good Friday Agreement, that they would be forced into a united Ireland against the will of the people of Northern Ireland.

Yet they realise now that a framework in which consent is guaranteed is also one in which basic rights of equality and justice are guaranteed, and that those who wish for a united Ireland are free to make that claim, provided it is democratically expressed, just as those who believe in the Union can make their claim.

It is all about belonging. The wish of unionists to belong to the UK. The wish of nationalists to belong to Ireland … Those urges to belong, divergent as they are, can live together more easily if we, Britain and the Irish Republic, can live closer together too.

Our ties are already rich and diverse: – the UK is the largest market for Irish goods. And you are our fifth most important market in the world; in culture, sport and academic life there is an enormous crossover. Our theatres are full of Irish plays. Our television is full of Irish actors and presenters. Your national football team has a few English accents too. Millions of Irish people live and work in Britain, and hundreds of thousands of us visit you every year.

The relationships across these islands are also changing in a significant way.

Our ministers and officials are increasingly consulting and coordinating systematically. We can do more. I believe we can transform our links if both sides are indeed ready to make the effort. For our part, we are.

None of this threatens our separate identities. Cooperation does not mean losing distinctiveness.

What I welcome above all is that, after keeping us apart for so long, Northern Ireland is now helping to bring us closer together. But I do not believe Northern Ireland can or should any longer define the relationship between us. Our common interests, what we can achieve together, go much, much wider than that.

Our two countries can look to the future with confidence in our separate ways. But we will be stronger and more prosperous working together.

That is my ambition. I know it is shared by the Taoiseach. I believe it is an ambition shared by both our nations. The 21st century awaits us. Let us confront its challenge with confidence, and together give our children the future they deserve.

Mary Harney
(b. 1953)

Mary Harney was born in Galway and studied economics at TCD, where she became the first female auditor of the Hist debating society. In 1977 she was appointed to the Senate, its youngest ever member. Elected to the Dáil in 1981 she resigned from Fianna Fáil in 1985 and co-founded the Progressive Democrats, becoming party leader in 1993. She became táiniste and minister for enterprise, trade and employment in 1997, and worked to attract direct investment from the US. By this time, the increasing emphasis on greater European integration was becoming an irritant in many EU member states, and Harney was vociferous in her opposition to the growth in European regulation and fiscal control.

> *'Ireland is now in a very real sense the gateway to Europe.'*

Mary Harney speaking at an EU Science and Innovation conference.

From her speech to the American Bar Association at the Law Society of Ireland, Blackhall Place, Dublin, 21 July 2000

History has bound this country very closely to the United States. Down the centuries millions of Irish people crossed the Atlantic in search of a new life in a new world. And that tradition of emigration laid the foundation for the strong social, economic and political ties between our two countries today.

Geography has placed this country on the edge of the European continent. One of our most significant achievements as an independent nation was our entry, almost 30 years ago, into what is now the European Union.

As Irish people our relationships with the United States and the European Union are complex. Geographically we are closer to Berlin than Boston. Spiritually we are probably a lot closer to Boston than Berlin.

Ireland is now in a very real sense the gateway to Europe. This is especially true for corporate America, whose companies are investing here in ever greater numbers and in ever greater volumes.

They see Ireland as an ideal base from which to attack the European market, the largest and most lucrative single market in the history of the world.

What really makes Ireland attractive to corporate America is the kind of economy we have created here. When Americans come here they find a country that believes in the incentive power of low taxation. They find a country that believes in economic liberalisation. They find a country that believes in essential regulation but not over-regulation. On looking further afield in Europe they find also that not every European country believes in all of these things.

It is a remarkable fact that a country with just one per cent of Europe's population accounts for 27 per cent of US greenfield investment in Europe.

Political and economic commentators sometimes pose a choice between what they see as the American way and the European way. They view the American way as being built on the rugged individualism of the original frontiersmen, an economic model that is heavily based on enterprise and incentive, on individual effort and with limited government intervention.

They view the European way as being built on a strong concern for social harmony and social inclusion, with governments being prepared to intervene strongly through the tax and regulatory systems to achieve their desired outcomes.

We in Ireland have tended to steer a course between the two but I think it is fair to say that we have sailed closer to the American shore than the European one.

Look at what we have done over the last 10 years. We have cut taxes on capital. We have cut taxes on corporate profits. We have cut taxes on personal incomes. The result has been an explosion in economic activity and Ireland is now the fastest-growing country in the developed world.

And did we have to pay some very high price for pursuing this policy option? Did we have to dismantle the welfare state? Did we have to abandon the concept of social inclusion? The answer is no: we didn't.

We have succeeded because even though we are members of the European Union, including now a currency union also, we still retain a very substantial freedom to control our political and economic destiny. Our taxation policy, for instance, is decided in Dublin, not Brussels.

This model works. It allows us to achieve our full economic potential for the first time in our history as an independent state.

It allows every other member state the freedom to chart its own course for social and economic progress.

And I say: if it ain't broke, don't fix it. There are some who want to create a more centralised Europe, a federal Europe, with key economic decisions being taken at Brussels level. I don't think that would be in Ireland's interests and I don't think it would be in Europe's interests either.

The fact is that Europe is not America and it never will be. The people of Europe are not united by a common language, common history and common tradition in the way that Americans are. During the next five years, for instance, the process of enlargement is likely to add a further half-a-dozen working languages to the European Union.

It is clear that there is such a thing as a single market for labour in America. Even with the advent of the single currency it is by no means clear that there is a single market for labour in Europe, or that one is likely to emerge any time soon.

I believe in a Europe of independent states, not a United States of Europe.

Gerry Adams
(b. 1948)

Born in Belfast, Gerry Adams joined Sinn Féin after leaving school. Taking part in the Catholic civil rights protests towards the end of the 1960s was the beginning of his 'defence' work. He was imprisoned by the British for most of the 1970s, after which he became more involved in politics. In 1983 he was elected leader of Sinn Féin, and to the British parliament, although he didn't take his seat. After the 1985 Anglo-Irish Agreement, Adams met with SDLP leader John Hume, and by the early 1990s, they had found common ground. With an IRA ceasefire in 1994, and the Belfast Agreement in 1998, multi-party devolved government in Northern Ireland became a reality. Adams was elected to the new Northern Ireland Assembly that year and served for more than 10 years. In 2011 he was elected to the Dáil, representing Louth.

'Our struggle has reached a defining moment.'

Gerry Adams on the campaign trail.

From a speech in Belfast, 6 April 2005

In the past I have defended the right of the IRA to engage in the armed struggle. I did so because there was no alternative for those who would not bend the knee, or turn a blind eye to oppression, or for those who wanted a national republic.

Now there is an alternative. I have clearly set out my view of what that alternative is. The way forward is by building political support for republican and democratic objectives across Ireland and by winning support for these goals internationally.

I want to use this occasion therefore to appeal to the leadership of Óglaigh na hÉireann to fully embrace and accept this alternative.

Can you take courageous initiatives which will achieve your aims by purely political and democratic activity?

I know full well that such truly historic decisions can only be taken in the aftermath of intense internal consultation. I ask that you initiate this as quickly as possible.

I understand fully that the IRA's most recent positive contribution to the peace process was in the context of a comprehensive agreement.

But I also hold the very strong view that republicans need to lead by example. There is no greater demonstration of this than in the IRA cessation in the summer of 1994.

Sinn Féin has demonstrated the ability to play a leadership role as part of a popular movement towards peace, equality and justice. We are totally committed to ending partition and to creating the conditions for unity and independence. Sinn Féin has the potential and capacity to become the vehicle for the attainment of republican objectives.

The Ireland we live in today is also a very different place from 15 years ago. There is now an all-Ireland agenda with huge potential. Nationalists and republicans have a confidence that will never again allow anyone to be treated as second-class citizens. Equality is our watchword. The catalyst for much of this change is the growing support for republicanism.

Of course, those who oppose change are not going to simply roll over. It will always be a battle a day between those who want maximum change and those who want to maintain the status quo.

But if republicans are to prevail, if the peace process is to be successfully concluded and Irish sovereignty and reunification secured, then we have to set the agenda – no one else is going to do that.

So, I also want to make a personal appeal to all of you – the women and men volunteers who have remained undefeated in the face of tremendous odds. Now is the time for you to step into the *Bearna Baoil* [the gap of danger] again; not as volunteers risking life and limb but as activists in a national movement towards independence and unity.

Such decisions will be far-reaching and difficult. But you never lacked courage in the past. Your courage is now needed for the future. It won't be easy. There are many problems to be resolved by the people of Ireland in the time ahead. Your ability as republican volunteers to rise to this challenge will mean that the two governments and others cannot easily hide from their obligations and their responsibility to resolve these problems.

Our struggle has reached a defining moment.

I am asking you to join me in seizing this moment, to intensify our efforts, to rebuild the peace process and decisively move our struggle forward.

Mary McAleese
(b. 1951)

Mary McAleese, barrister, academic and television presenter, was born in Belfast. In 1997 she ran for the Irish presidency as the Fianna Fáil candidate and served two consecutive terms. In 2005 the Irish government decided to reinstitute the military aspect of the Easter Sunday parade in Dublin, in order 'to reclaim the spirit of 1916', which many felt had been hijacked by the IRA campaign in Northern Ireland. Public opinion was divided, but the huge turnout at the 2006 parade showed that a majority were in favour. In an address earlier that year, McAleese delivered a rousing defence of the idea of honouring those who had taken part in the 1916 Rising.

'We are where freedom has brought us.'

From a speech at University College Cork, 27 January 2006

With each passing year, post-Rising Ireland reveals itself and we, who are of this strong, independent and high-achieving Ireland, would do well to ponder the extent to which today's freedoms, values, ambitions and success rest on that perilous and militarily doomed undertaking of nine decades ago, and on the words of [the] Proclamation. Clearly its fundamental idea was freedom, or in the words of the Proclamation, 'the right of the Irish people to the ownership of Ireland', but it was also a very radical assertion of the kind of republic a liberated Ireland should become. 'The Republic guarantees religious and civil liberty, equal rights and equal opportunities to all its citizens and declares its resolve to pursue the happiness and prosperity of the whole nation and all of its parts cherishing all the children of the nation equally.' It spoke of a Parliament 'representative of the whole people of Ireland and elected by the suffrages of all her men and women' – this at a time when Westminster was still refusing to concede the vote to women on the basis that to do so would be to give in to terrorism. To our 21st-century ears these words seem a good fit for our modern democracy.

Yet 90 years ago, even 40 years ago, they seemed hopelessly naïve, and their long-term intellectual power was destined to be overlooked, as interest was focused on the emotionally charged political power of the Rising and the renewed nationalist fervour it evoked.

In the longer term the apparent naïveté of the words of the Proclamation has filled out into a widely shared political philosophy of equality and social inclusion in tune with the contemporary spirit of democracy, human rights, equality and anti-confessionalism. Read now in the light of the liberation of women, the development of social partnership, the focus on rights and equality, the ending of the special position of the Catholic church, to mention but a few, we see a much more coherent, and wider reaching, intellectual event than may have previously been noted.

The kind of Ireland the heroes of the rising aspired to was based on an inclusivity that, famously, would 'cherish all the children of the nation equally – oblivious of the differences which have divided a minority from the majority in the past'.

In 1916, Ireland was a small nation attempting to gain independence from one of Europe's many powerful empires. In the 19th century an English radical described the occupation of India as a system of 'outdoor relief' for the younger sons of the upper classes. The administration of Ireland was not very different, being carried on as a process of continuous conversation around the fire in the Kildare Street Club by past pupils of public schools. It was no way to run a country.

The leaders of the Rising were not attempting to establish an isolated and segregated territory of 'ourselves alone', as the phrase 'sinn féin' is so often mistranslated, but a free country in which we ourselves could take responsibility for our own destiny, a country that could stand up for itself, have its own distinct perspective, pull itself up by its bootstraps, and be counted with respect, among the free nations of Europe and the world.

I have a strong impression that to its enemies, both in Ireland and abroad, Irish nationalism looked like a version of the imperialism it opposed, a sort of 'imperialism lite' through which Ireland would attempt to be what the Great European powers were – the domination of one cultural and ethnic tradition over others. It is easy to see how they might have fallen into that mistaken view, but mistaken they were. Irish nationalism, from the start, was a multilateral enterprise, attempting to escape the dominance of a single class and, in our case, a largely foreign class, into a wider world. Those who think of Irish nationalists as narrow, miss, for example, the membership many of them had of a universal church which brought them into contact with a vastly wider segment of the world than that open to even the most travelled imperial English gentleman. Many of the leaders had experience of the Americas, and in particular of North America with its vibrant attachment to liberty and democracy. Others of them were active participants in the international working-class movements of their day.

Paradoxically, in the longer run, 1916 arguably set in motion a calming of old conflicts with new concepts and confidence which, as they mature and take shape, stand us in good stead today.

In the hearts of those who took part in the Rising, in what was then an undivided Ireland, was an unshakeable belief that whatever our personal political or religious perspectives, there was a huge potential for an Ireland in which loyalist, republican, unionist, nationalist, Catholic, Protestant, atheist, agnostic pulled together to build a shared future, owned by one and all. That's a longer term to conjure with but, for now, reflecting back on the sacrifices of the heroes of 1916 and the gallingly unjust world that was their context, I look at my own context and its threads of connection to theirs. I am humbled, excited and grateful to live in one of the world's most respected, admired and successful democracies, a country with an identifiably distinctive voice in Europe and in the world, an Irish republic, a sovereign independent state to use the words of the Proclamation. We are where freedom has brought us. A tough journey, but more than vindicated by our contemporary context. Like every nation that had to wrench its freedom from the reluctant grip of empire we have our idealistic and heroic founding fathers and mothers, our Davids and their Goliaths. That small band who proclaimed the Rising inhabited a sea of death, an unspeakable time of the most profligate worldwide waste of human life. Yet their deaths rise far above the clamour – their voices insistent still.

Ian Paisley
(1926–2014)

Founder of the evangelical Free Presbyterian Church in 1951, Ian Paisley's political career spanned almost 40 years. A committed loyalist, he was opposed to any form of compromise with nationalists – he personified the 'Ulster says no' campaign. After decades of political agitation and violence, the Belfast Agreement introduced the possibility of a positive way forward in Northern Ireland. However, with politicians on either side still at a stalemate in 2007, the British government offered a huge investment package if both sides would agree. Paisley met with Gerry Adams for the first time ever and they agreed to share power. On 8 May 2007 Paisley was sworn in as Northern Ireland's first minister, with Sinn Féin's Martin McGuinness as deputy first minister. They got on so well together that they were known as 'the chuckle brothers'.

> *'Today we have begun to plant*
> *and we await the harvest.'*

From his speech at Stormont at his swearing in as first minister, 8 May 2007

Today at long last we are starting upon the road – I emphasise starting – which I believe will take us to lasting peace in our province. I have not changed my unionism, the Union of Northern Ireland within the United Kingdom, which I believe is today stronger than ever.

We are making this declaration, we are all aiming to build a Northern Ireland in which we can all live together in peace, being equal under the law and equally subject to the law.

I welcome the pledge we have all taken to that effect today. That is the rock foundation upon which we must build.

Today we salute Ulster's honoured and unageing dead – the innocent victims, that gallant band, members of both religions, Protestant and Roman Catholic, strong in their allegiance to their differing political beliefs, unionist and nationalist, male and female, children and adults, all innocent victims of the terrible conflict.

In the shadows of the evenings and in the sunrise of the mornings we hail their gallantry and heroism. It cannot and will not be erased from our memories.

Nor can we forget those who continue to bear the scars of suffering and whose bodies have been robbed of sight, robbed of hearing, robbed of limbs. Yes, and we must shed the silent and bitter tear for those whose loved ones' bodies have not yet been returned.

Let me read to you the words of Deirdre Speer, who lost her police officer father in the struggle.

Remember me! Remember me!

My sculptured glens where crystal rivers run,

My purple mountains, misty in the sun,

My coastlines, little changed since time begun,

I gave you birth.

Remember me! Remember me!

Though battle-scarred and weary I abide.

When you speak of history, say my name with pride.

I am Ulster.

In politics, as in life, it is a truism that no one can ever have 100 per cent of what they desire. They must make a verdict when they believe they have achieved enough to move things forward. Unlike at any other time I believe we are now able to make progress.

I have sensed a great sigh of relief amongst all our people who want the hostility to be replaced with neighbourliness.

The great king Solomon said:

To everything there is a season, and a time to every purpose under heaven.

A time to be born and a time to die.

A time to plant and time to pluck up that which is planted.

A time to kill and a time to heal.

A time to break down and a time to build up.

A time to get and a time to lose.

A time to keep and a time to cast away.

A time to love and a time to hate.

A time of war and a time of peace.

I believe that Northern Ireland has come to a time of peace, a time when hate will no longer rule.

How good it will be to be part of a wonderful healing in our province.

Today we have begun to plant and we await the harvest.

Barack Obama
(b. 1961)

The 44th President of the United States, Barack Obama served three terms in the Illinois Senate and was elected to the US Senate in 2004. He was elected US President on the Democrat ticket in 2008, and was returned for a second term in 2012. He was awarded the Nobel Peace Prize in 2009. His liberal presidency promoted gun control and healthcare reform and normalised relations with Cuba. In 2011 Obama, who had an Irish great-great-great-grandfather, made a state visit to Ireland. He addressed the nation at College Green in Dublin.

'Is féidir linn. Yes we can.'

From his College Green address on 23 May 2011.

Earlier today Michelle and I visited Moneygall where we saw my ancestral home and dropped by the local pub. And it was remarkable to see the small town where a young shoemaker named Falmouth Kearney, my great-great-great grandfather, my grandfather's grandfather, lived his early life.

And he left during the Great Hunger, as so many Irish did, to seek a new life in the New World. He travelled by ship to New York, where he entered himself into the records as a labourer. He married an American girl from Ohio. They settled in the Midwest. They started a family.

It's a familiar story because it's one lived and cherished by Americans of all backgrounds. It's integral to our national identity. It's who we are, a nation of immigrants from all around the world.

But standing there in Moneygall I couldn't help but think how heartbreaking it must have been for that great-great-great grandfather of mine, and so many others, to part. To watch Donegal coasts and Dingle cliffs recede. To leave behind all they knew in hopes that something better lay over the horizon.

When people like Falmouth boarded those ships, they often did so with no family, no friends, no money, nothing to sustain their journey but faith – faith in the Almighty; faith in the idea of America; faith that it was a place where you could be prosperous, you could be free, you could think and talk and worship as you pleased, a place where you could make it if you tried.

And as they worked and struggled and sacrificed and sometimes experienced great discrimination, to build that better life for the next generation, they passed on that faith to their children and to their children's children – an inheritance that their great-great-great grandchildren still carry with them. We call it the American Dream.

For America's sake, we're grateful so many others from this land took that chance, as well. Never has a nation so small inspired so much in another. Irish signatures are on our founding documents. Irish blood was spilled on our battlefields. Irish sweat built our great cities. Our spirit is eternally refreshed by Irish story and Irish song; our public life by the humour and heart and dedication of servants with names like Kennedy and Reagan, O'Neill and Moynihan. So you could say there's always been a little green behind the red, white and blue.

When the father of our country, George Washington, needed an army, it was the fierce fighting of your sons that caused the British official to lament, 'We have lost America through the Irish'.

When Abraham Lincoln struggled to preserve our young union, more than 100,000 Irish and Irish Americans joined the cause, with units like the Irish Brigade charging into battle – green flags with gold harp waving alongside our star-spangled banner.

And when an Iron Curtain fell across this continent and our way of life was challenged, it was our first Irish President – our first Catholic President, John F. Kennedy, who made us believe 50 years ago this week that mankind could do something as big and bold and ambitious as walk on the moon. He made us dream again.

I think we all realise that both of our nations have faced great trials in recent years, including recessions so severe that many of our people are still trying to fight their way out. Those of us who are parents wonder what it will mean for our children and young people like so many who are here today. Will you see the same progress we've seen since we were your age? Will you inherit futures as big and as bright as the ones that we inherited? Will your dreams remain alive in our time?

This nation has faced those questions before: When your land couldn't feed those who tilled it; when the boats leaving these shores held some of your brightest minds; when brother fought against brother. Yours is a history frequently marked by the greatest of trials and the deepest of sorrows. But yours is also a history of proud and defiant endurance. Of a nation that kept alive the flame of knowledge in dark ages; that overcame occupation and outlived fallow fields; that triumphed over its Troubles – of a resilient people who beat all the odds.

And, Ireland, as trying as these times are, I know our future is still as big and as bright as our children expect it to be. We're people, the Irish and Americans, who never stop imagining a brighter future, even in bitter times. We're people who make that future happen through hard work, and through sacrifice, through investing in those things that matter most, like family and community.

We remember, in the words made famous by one of your greatest poets that 'in dreams begins responsibility'.

This is a nation that met its responsibilities by choosing to apply the lessons of your own past to assume a heavier burden of responsibility on the world stage. And today, a people who once knew the pain of an empty stomach now feed those who hunger abroad. Ireland is working hand in hand with the United States to make sure that hungry mouths are fed around the world – because we remember those times. We know what crippling poverty can be like, and we want to make sure we're helping others.

You're a people who modernised and can now stand up for those who can't yet stand up for themselves. And this is a nation that met its responsibilities – and inspired the entire world – by choosing to see past the scars of violence and mistrust to forge a lasting peace on this island.

In dreams begin responsibility. And embracing that responsibility, working toward it, overcoming the cynics and the naysayers and those who say 'you can't' – that's what makes dreams real. That's what Falmouth Kearney did when he got on that boat, and that's what so many generations of Irish men and women have done here in this spectacular country. That is something we can point to and show our children, Irish and American alike.

This little country, that inspires the biggest things – your best days are still ahead. And, Ireland, if anyone ever says otherwise, if anybody ever tells you that your problems are too big, or your challenges are too great, that we can't do something, that we shouldn't even try – think about all that we've done together. Remember that whatever hardships the winter may bring, springtime is always just around the corner. And if they keep on arguing with you, just respond with a simple creed: *Is féidir linn.* Yes, we can. Yes, we can. *Is féidir linn.*

For all you've contributed to the character of the United States of America and the spirit of the world, thank you. And may God bless the eternal friendship between our two great nations.

Panti Bliss
(b. 1986)

Rory O'Neill, also known as the drag artist, Miss Panti Bliss, was born in Ballinrobe, County Mayo and studied at Dun Laoghaire College of Art. He hosts the annual Dublin gay pride celebrations and performs as a drag artist at various venues. In January 2014 he appeared on RTÉ television on a chat show – when the subject of homophobia was raised, he named several journalists he believed to be homophobic. RTÉ paid the journalists off when they threatened to take legal action. The incident became something of a cause célèbre and was discussed by the Irish government and in the European Parliament. The following month O'Neill/Panti gave a 'Noble Call' speech at the Abbey Theatre in response to the controversy.

'And that feels oppressive.'

From his Noble Call address at the Abbey Theatre, 1 February 2014

Hello. My name is Panti and I am a drag queen, a performer, and an accidental and occasional gay rights activist.

And as you may have already gathered, I am also painfully middle-class. My father was a country vet, I went to a nice school, and afterwards to that most middle-class of institutions – art college. And although this may surprise some of you, I have always managed to find gainful employment in my chosen field – gender discombobulation.

So the grinding, abject poverty so powerfully displayed in tonight's performance is something I can thankfully say I have no experience of.

But oppression is something I can relate to. Oh, I'm not comparing my experience to Dublin workers of 1913, but I do know what it feels like to be put in your place.

Have you ever been standing at a pedestrian crossing when a car drives by and in it are a bunch of lads, and they lean out the window and they shout 'Fag!' and throw a milk carton at you?

Now it doesn't really hurt. It's just a wet carton and anyway they're right – I am a fag. But it feels oppressive.

When it really does hurt, is afterwards. Afterwards I wonder and worry and obsess over what was it about me, what was it they saw in me? What was it that gave me away? And I hate myself for wondering that. It feels oppressive and the next time I'm at a pedestrian crossing I check myself to see what is it about me that 'gives the gay away' and I check myself to make sure I'm not doing it this time.

Have any of you ever come home in the evening and turned on the television and there is a panel of people – nice people, respectable people, smart people, the kind of people who make good neighbourly neighbours and write for newspapers. And they are having a reasoned debate about you. About what kind of a person you are, about whether you are capable of being a good parent, about whether you want to destroy marriage, about whether you are safe around children, about whether God herself thinks you are an abomination, about whether in fact you are 'intrinsically disordered'. And even the nice TV presenter lady who you feel like you know thinks it's perfectly OK that they are all having this reasonable debate about who you are and what rights you 'deserve'. And that feels oppressive.

Have you ever been on a crowded train with your gay friend and a small part of you is cringing because he is being SO gay and you find yourself trying to compensate by butching up or nudging the conversation onto 'straighter' territory? This is you who have spent 35 years trying to be the best gay possible and yet still a small part of you is embarrassed by his gayness.

And I hate myself for that. And that feels oppressive. And when I'm standing at the pedestrian lights I am checking myself.

Have you ever gone into your favourite neighbourhood café with the paper that you buy every day, and you open it up and inside is a 500-word opinion written by a nice middle-class woman, the kind of woman who probably gives to charity, the kind of woman that you would be happy to leave your children with. And she is arguing so reasonably about whether you should be treated less than everybody else, arguing that you should be given fewer rights than everybody else. And when the woman at the next table gets up and excuses herself to squeeze by you with a smile you wonder, 'Does she think that about me too?'

And that feels oppressive. And you go outside and you stand at the pedestrian crossing and you check yourself and I hate myself for that.

Have you ever turned on the computer and seen videos of people just like you in far away countries, and countries not far away at all, being beaten and imprisoned and tortured and murdered because they are just like you?

And that feels oppressive.

Three weeks ago I was on the television and I said that I believed that people who actively campaign for gay people to be treated less or differently are, in my gay opinion, homophobic. Some people, people who actively campaign for gay people to be treated less under the law took great exception at this characterisation and threatened legal action against me and RTÉ. RTÉ, in its wisdom, decided incredibly quickly to hand over a huge sum of money to make it go away. I haven't been so lucky.

And for the last three weeks I have been lectured by heterosexual people about what homophobia is and who should be allowed identify it. Straight people – ministers, senators, lawyers, journalists – have lined up to tell me what homophobia is and what I am allowed to feel oppressed by. People who have never experienced homophobia in their lives, people who have never checked themselves at a pedestrian crossing, have told me that unless I am being thrown in prison or herded onto a cattle train, then it is not homophobia.

And that feels oppressive.

So now Irish gay people find ourselves in a ludicrous situation where not only are we not allowed to say publicly what we feel oppressed by, we are not even allowed to think it because our definition has been disallowed by our betters.

And for the last three weeks I have been denounced from the floor of parliament to newspaper columns to the seething morass of internet commentary for 'hate speech' because I dared to use the word 'homophobia'. And a jumped-up queer like me should know that the word 'homophobia' is no longer available to gay people. Which is a spectacular and neat Orwellian trick because now it turns out that gay people are not the victims of homophobia – homophobes are.

But I want to say that it is not true. I don't hate you.

I do, it is true, believe that almost all of you are probably homophobes. But I'm a homophobe. It would be incredible if we weren't. To grow up in a society that is overwhelmingly homophobic and to escape unscathed would be miraculous. So I don't hate you because you are homophobic. I actually admire you. I admire you because most of you are only a bit homophobic. Which all things considered is pretty good going.

But I do sometimes hate myself. I hate myself because I fucking check myself while standing at pedestrian crossings. And sometimes I hate you for doing that to me.

But not right now. Right now, I like you all very much for giving me a few moments of your time. And I thank you for it.

Michael D. Higgins
(b. 1941)

A native of Limerick, Ireland's ninth president is a poet, sociologist, writer and broadcaster. He was minister for arts, culture and the Gaeltacht from 1993 to 1997. As President of the Labour Party from 2003, he accepted the party's nomination for the presidential election in 2011. Ireland celebrated the centenary of the 1916 Rising in April 2016. In March the President addressed the relatives of those who had participated in it.

'Our nation has journeyed many miles.'

From his address at the RDS, Dublin, 26 March 2016

Across a distance of time there is the danger that we might lose the human essence of the lives of the men and women who changed the course of our history, or perhaps at a distance be inclined to interpret their actions solely through the prism of competing accounts of major political or constitutional change. Tonight we have the opportunity to give correct place to the intimate human dimension of the Easter Rising and the sacrifices made by so many of those who helped to build our nation.

Those sacrifices by your forebears are, for all Irish citizens, a source of inspiration and patriotic pride, but they are for you, in addition, personal stories of family experience, choices made that had special meaning and consequences for your families.

The key actors in the Rising were not abstract or mythical figures; they were living, and particularly conscious and engaged men and women. They were poets, academics, journalists and civil servants; city clerks and shopkeepers; Catholics and Protestants, whose voices made the call for a new and re-imagined Ireland.

Today we view the Rising as being synonymous with republicanism, but that of course was not a dominant ideology at the time; even if it was understood, and deliberately included in the Proclamation by Pearse and Connolly who were very well aware of its historical and contemporary significance and of its emancipatory promise.

The loss of Patrick Pearse and James Connolly, who had brought an egalitarian, workers' rights emphasis into the Citizen Army Volunteer relationship, whose coming together is reflected in the language of the Proclamation, would become all the more evident in years that followed with the difficulties that would obstruct the drafting of the Democratic Programme of the Dáil in 1919, the minimalism of the 1922 Constitution which could not carry the language of Pearse and Connolly, and indeed the deep institutional conservatism of the early decades of the state.

The Ireland of the early 20th century was a complex place where the shops, restaurants and back rooms of radical Dublin were alive with the conversations of a dynamic mixture of feminists, socialists, radicals, nationalists, anti-imperialists and the many other ideologists compelled, in their different ways, to dream of a new and better Ireland.

All of the participants in 1916 had come to perceive and recoil from what was a constant theme in the assumptions of the Imperialist mind: that those dominated in any colony such as Ireland were lesser in human terms, in language, culture and politics.

It is critical to our understanding of the Rising that we view it too in the broader historical context of World War l. This was, together with the Lockout of 1913, an important pretext to the Rising. By the early 20th century, a pinnacle of imperialist expectation and arrogance had been reached, and the unassailability of the great European Empires, assured a century earlier at Vienna, was now under attack. The First World War and its rhetoric reinforced a perception that imperialism was drawing its final breath; after all six Empires entered the war, only two would emerge.

Culture was a central element of the Rising and an inspiration for those who took part. In the years leading up to Easter 1916, the Irish had become an increasingly literate people, giving rise to an extensive readership of newspapers which allowed an alternative culture to emerge in the shape of provocative and radical Irish journalism.

The Irish literary revival was part of a profoundly progressive movement, which had seen, in rapid succession, the founding of the Land League, the Gaelic Athletic Association and the Gaelic League, as a generation of Irish men and women sought through such organisations to simultaneously retrieve their heritage, and fashion an alternative Ireland. Myriad and intertwined connections existed between these groups at both executive and grass roots levels, and it was such mutual affiliations that created the networks of the emerging political movement that was to lead us into Easter 1916.

W. B. Yeats, Jack Yeats, James Joyce, George Russell, Sean O'Casey – the richness of the cultural milieu of the time is stunning. These were artists and thinkers who were generous and committed to the life of the public and the life of the community. Nationalist, republican, socialist, feminist, internationalist – the great men and women of the period typically lived many of these roles. They dreamed of creating something new and radical in Ireland, something which would also be continuous with a distinct Irish culture and history.

All of these strands of the Rising are present in the idealism of the Proclamation which offers us a generous social and political vision, one that can still inspire us today. We should never forget that it was addressed too to the nation's women as well as its men in equal terms, two years before women over 30 were allowed to vote, as it called forth a Republic that would guarantee: 'religious and civil liberty, equal rights and equal opportunities to all its citizens'.

During the passage from the Proclamation to the 1930s that egalitarian emphasis would weaken. Women would have to struggle for their equality and in that they would invoke the most direct connections with the women of 1916. This inheritance they invoked particularly in the debate on Bunreacht na hÉireann in 1937.

Our nation has journeyed many miles from the shell shocked and burning Dublin of 1916. We can see that in many respects we have not fully achieved the dreams and ideals for which our forebears gave so much.

A democracy is always and must always be a work in progress. We must ensure that our journey into the future is a collective one; one in which the homeless, the migrant, the disadvantaged, the marginalised and each and every citizen can find homes, are fellow travellers on our journey which includes all of the multitude of voices that together speak of, and for, a new Ireland born out of contemporary imagination and challenges.

So this evening, let us look to our past in a way that is emancipatory and transformative.

Let us remember, with respect, not only those who have called us here today, or those leaders whose names are indelibly etched into the history books of Ireland, but also all those who lost their lives during the 1916 Rising.

Picture credits

The publisher gratefully acknowledges the following image copyright holders. All images are copyright © individual rights holders unless stated otherwise. Every effort has been made to trace copyright holders, or copyright holders not mentioned here. If there have been any errors or omissions, the publisher would be happy to rectify this in any reprint.